BEYOND

REFORM

Systemic Shifts *Toward* Personalized Learning

Lindsay Unified School District

Foreword by Robert J. Marzano

MARZANO
— Research —

555 North Morton Street
Bloomington, IN 47404
888.849.0851
FAX: 866.801.1447

email: info@marzanoresearch.com
marzanoresearch.com

Visit **marzanoresearch.com/reproducibles** to download the free reproducibles in this book.

Printed in the United States of America

Library of Congress Control Number: 2016958918

ISBN: 978-1-943360-11-6 (paperback)

21 20 19 18 17   1 2 3 4 5

Text and Cover Designer: Laura Cox

Acknowledgments

The authors would like to acknowledge and extend a special thank you for the support of the Lindsay Unified parents and families, the Lindsay Unified Board of Trustees, the Lindsay Unified learners and learning facilitators, and the Lindsay Leaders.

Visit **marzanoresearch.com/reproducibles** to download the free reproducibles in this book.

Table of Contents

Lindsay Unified School District

Authors

Tom Rooney, Superintendent, Lindsay Unified School District
Lana Brown, Deputy Superintendent, Lindsay Unified School District
Barry Sommer, Director of Advancement, Lindsay Unified School District
Amalia Lopez, Learning Facilitator and Curriculum Design Specialist, Lindsay Unified School District

---

Contributing Researchers

Dr. Leslie Poynor, Research Associate, WestEd
Dr. Katie Strom, Assistant Professor, California State University, East Bay
Dr. Eric Haas, Senior Research Associate, WestEd

Contributing Editors

Beatrice McGarvey, Consultant, McGarvey Educational Associates
Bobbie Velasquez, Secretary to the Superintendent, Lindsay Unified School District
Janet Kliegl, Former Superintendent, Lindsay Unified School District
Joy Soares, Director of College and Career Readiness, Tulare County Office of Education
Nikolaus Namba, Principal, Lindsay Unified School District
Brian Griffin, Director of Personalized Learning, Lindsay Unified School District
Cinnamon Scheufele, Principal, Lindsay Unified School District
Charles Schwahn, Consultant, Schwahn Leadership Associates

About Marzano Research

Marzano Research is a joint venture between Solution Tree and Dr. Robert J. Marzano. Marzano Research combines Dr. Marzano's more than forty years of educational research with continuous action research in all major areas of schooling in order to provide effective and accessible instructional strategies, leadership strategies, and classroom assessment strategies that are always at the forefront of best practice. By providing such an all-inclusive research-into-practice resource center, Marzano Research provides teachers and principals with the tools they need to effect profound and immediate improvement in student achievement.

Foreword

by Robert J. Marzano

Every few decades or so, a paradigm shift has the potential to occur. Most of the time, these potential shifts do not fully manifest—usually because there are no schools or districts innovative and brave enough to provide a concrete manifestation of the change in its purest form.

Several years ago, performance-based education became an "idea whose time had come." All the pieces were in place conceptually, and advances were being made on the specific elements that must exist to have a true performance-based system. While a number of schools and districts attempted to become pure exemplars of such a system, none were successful at the requisite level to motivate others to follow—that is, until Lindsay Unified entered the scene.

In a relatively short period of time, Lindsay Unified School District transformed its system into one that can and should become the model for K–12 education for the next several decades. It was not an easy journey. The district learned many lessons about what to do and what *not* to do. Fortunately, in this book, Tom Rooney and his colleagues have laid out the specifics of both.

They begin by inspiring the reader with a vision of what schools and districts can do right now and what education can look like in the future. Their anecdotes about changes in students, schools, and the community at large are both informative and compelling.

They then provide a concrete model of a necessary strategic design process that involves five foundational sets of questions:

1. Why do we exist as an organization?

2. What are the core values that will govern how we will interact with one another?

3. What are the guiding principles that will inform our decision making around teaching, learning, learners, and community?

4. What is our vision for the future related to learning, curricula, instruction, assessment, technology, personnel, leadership, and stakeholders?

5. What is the description of our graduates? What do they need to know, be able to do, and be like to lead successful lives when they graduate?

Although the authors do not state it directly, it is easy to infer that they believe the initial internal soul searching and goal setting are foundational to effective reform. Without them, implementation of the specifics will most probably falter with the first significant obstacle.

With these questions as a backdrop, the authors provide concrete guidance on implementation issues that include creating a new culture, leading a paradigm shift, empowering personnel, transforming curricula and assessment, transforming teaching, and transforming community relationships.

In all, this book provides insight into both the big picture and the fine brushstrokes needed to move a system from traditional education to a high-functioning performance-based system. This book is definitely a must-read for anyone interested in moving his or her school or district to the new paradigm of K–12 education.

Introduction

Many districts have experienced difficulty meeting the needs of increasingly diverse student populations and preparing graduates for postsecondary education and the 21st century workforce. Lindsay Unified School District set out to meet this challenge by shifting from a traditional time-based education system, in which students are expected to conform to a one-size-fits-all pace, to a performance-based model, titled as the Performance Based System in Lindsay Unified, in which learners progress only when they have demonstrated mastery. The district's complex, multiyear journey, which continues to this day, has entailed fully dismantling the prior system and transforming structures, processes, and roles—all driven by a major paradigm shift in conceptions of teaching and learning.

In chapter 1, readers meet Yesenia and Junior, two former Lindsay Unified students whose education outcomes are typical of many students who went through Lindsay schools prior to the shift in the district's approach to teaching and learning. Students like Yesenia and Junior helped to catalyze the district's commitment to implementing its Performance Based System in order to better serve all students. Throughout the remaining chapters, readers meet other learners whose schooling experiences were transformed by the Performance Based System.

Chapter 1 also provides an overview of the broader Lindsay community and its learners, explains the need for change, and reviews some of the district's early reform efforts, which eventually led to the decision to shift to the Performance Based System. Chapter 2 describes the transformation of the district's culture, which has been central to the success that it has experienced over the last several years. The remaining chapters detail the process of change and aspects of the Lindsay system, including leadership, personnel, curricula and assessment, teaching and learning, and community. These chapters discuss the vision for each component and the steps taken to achieve that vision.

In all, *Beyond Reform* unpacks Lindsay Unified's vision for learning, articulates the steps that it has taken toward achieving that vision, and shares lessons learned thus far. This book was conceived as a support for schools, districts, and stakeholder groups that might wish to adopt the innovations and promising practices of Lindsay's districtwide transformation effort. The intended audience includes a broad range of educators and leaders in primary and secondary education, as well as education foundations, policymakers, and others who are committed to ensuring that all students are successful learners.

CHAPTER 1

Preparing for Change

Yesenia
Lindsay High School, Class of 2008

Yesenia, whose parents are migrant workers, finished her required courses in time to graduate in the middle of her senior year. She was full of smiles at the small December ceremony, but soon thereafter her joy turned to anxiety as she realized that she had graduated without purpose or direction and had no idea what her future looked like.

The oldest of seven children, Yesenia felt the weight of being both a role model and a provider for her siblings. Now she was overtaken with despair, worrying that the poverty with which her parents struggled would characterize her own future as well. In January, Yesenia returned to campus at Lindsay High School, asking to see the principal. She sat in one of the blue plastic waiting-room chairs with tears streaming down her face.

"Yesenia, what's wrong?" the principal asked when he saw her. "You just graduated!"

She looked up miserably. "That's just it," she said. "I'm done with school, but I don't know what to do."

Yesenia left the office that day uncertain about what to do, and the principal realized that yet another student had been allowed to graduate without a viable plan for life.

Junior
Lindsay High School, Class of 2007

On a hot day at the end of June, Lindsay High School's newly appointed principal unlocked the door to his office for the very first time. He entered, set down the boxes he was carrying, and began to unpack, until he heard a knock at his door. Looking up, he saw the school secretary, who said, "Mr. Gonzales is here with his son, Junior, to see you."

Smiling, the principal shook hands with them and asked what he could do for them.

"Well, Junior graduated from Lindsay High School just a couple of days ago," Mr. Gonzales began.

Turning to Junior, the principal said, "Congratulations. So what are you going to be doing next?"

"That's the problem," Mr. Gonzales said, shaking his head sadly. Gesturing to the copy of the Foothills Sun-Gazette *on a nearby shelf, he asked the principal to hand it to him.*

Unsure of what to expect, the principal handed the paper to the father, who, in turn, passed it to Junior.

"Go ahead, son. Read this article in the newspaper."

Junior quietly held the folded newspaper, his eyes downcast and nervous. "You are a graduate of Lindsay High School," urged his father. "Read it."

Junior looked up at his father and, in a low voice, said, "Dad, you know I can't read."

The Lindsay Unified School District Context

Lindsay Unified School District, which serves more than four thousand learners from the city of Lindsay and the surrounding communities, is located in California's agriculturally rich San Joaquin Valley. Lindsay is a small, rural community known for its citrus orchards and olive groves. Home to a large population of immigrant families, Lindsay is composed of a high percentage of families living below the federal poverty level, many with low levels of literacy in English and low levels of parent education. Many of the district's learners come from migrant families who work in the surrounding fields and production areas. In 2016, 83 percent of Lindsay learners were from low-income families, and more than 550 learners were legally considered homeless. Approximately 85 percent of Lindsay learners were eligible for free or reduced-price meals (although in practice, 100 percent of Lindsay learners receive them). Ninety-three percent were Latino, and approximately 50 percent were English learners (California Department of Education, 2016; California Department of Education Data Reporting Office, n.d.).

These statistics are the result of a demographic shift within the district. In the late 1990s, the poverty level began to rise in Lindsay. Middle- and upper-class families began to leave, and the number of immigrant families increased dramatically. As the new community members began enrolling their children in school, Lindsay Unified saw exponential growth in its number of English learners (ELs). This change presented a major dilemma for Lindsay Unified leaders and teachers, most of whom had little or no preparation to teach ELs. Many resisted the idea that they should be required to teach these learners, while others had the will but not the capacity or resources to successfully do so. In reference to this learner population, the superintendent at the time said, "The truth is that back in 1998, we didn't know how to meet their needs."

English learners were not the only group that needed to be better served; Lindsay Unified's overall Academic Performance Index (API) scores were some of the lowest in the state (California Department of Education, 2001). Graduation rates were in the low 70th percentile of California districts, and, between 1999 and 2009, nine of the district's eleven high school valedictorians required remedial courses in college.

The need to better serve Lindsay learners was obvious, but the system was broken on multiple levels. School facilities were in abysmal shape. Budgetary practices were questionable at best. The district had become a revolving door for teachers; more than half of the staff at any given school were new each year. Lindsay Unified's board of trustees (that is, its board of education) and the teachers' union were involved in a dispute over salaries and binding arbitration, and there was talk of a strike. Attracting quality leadership at both the school and district levels had become almost impossible. These trends painted a clear picture for district leaders: the traditional system was failing Lindsay learners.

Early Transformations

Early efforts to reform the district's education system began in the late 1990s and addressed the immediate systemic and organizational issues that needed to be resolved before the district could effectively grapple with deeper academic challenges. The first steps included building leadership capacity. As a key early strategy, the district hired a new assistant superintendent who could help address the district's cultural and academic challenges and repair relationships among staff. The new assistant superintendent, a Latina educator and a former migrant learner herself, entered the district as an established and well-respected figure in the broader Lindsay community.

In the dispute between the board of trustees and the union, the superintendent acted as a mediator, negotiating a compromise between the two sides. The compromise included the board updating salary schedules to make positions more attractive to outside candidates. The administration also developed a centralized process for new hires that allowed the district to strategically select the right people for pivotal positions, including teachers, vice principals, and district personnel who directly impacted teaching and learning practices. Further changes in leadership included hiring a new chief business officer and a new human relations director. Recognizing that new leadership was needed at the site level, the district replaced several principals with experienced school leaders who had strong instructional backgrounds, were effective problem solvers, and had proven track records of leading substantial and meaningful change. During this same period, board members received training to help them better understand their roles and responsibilities as trustees.

With the intent of helping to build new relationships and trust among staff members, district leaders established informal monthly meetings for discussions with teachers, support personnel, and union representatives. These meetings set the stage for relaxed exchanges of information and ideas. Fostering these new relationships proved to be essential for establishing the necessary foundation of trust for the next set of changes, which focused on improving academic achievement.

In the early 2000s, additional reform efforts continued, focused on the most pressing academic challenges for Lindsay learners: language acquisition and literacy. Too many learners were not reading at grade level, and too many teachers did not know how to teach them to read. To address this issue, the district adopted Reading Recovery, an individualized literacy intervention program designed to help first graders whose reading skills were below grade level. Reading Recovery instilled in staff a new sense of urgency to improve learner achievement; they began using assessments and data to better understand individual learner needs and to inform instructional practices. Because it is so individualized, Reading Recovery served as a stepping stone toward the Performance Based System that Lindsay Unified had begun envisioning for the whole district. Learners who had previously fallen through the cracks were rapidly improving in their language acquisition and literacy, and, as teachers saw evidence of learner success, resistance to instructional changes began to dissipate.

Although Reading Recovery was yielding results for struggling young readers, the district knew that more improvement was needed for learners across grades and content areas. Lindsay Unified's broader instructional improvement efforts incorporated a set of research-based strategies, which, if implemented correctly, "have a high probability of enhancing student achievement for all students in all subject areas at all grade levels" (Marzano, Pickering, & Pollock, 2001, p. 7). These strategies and their purposes include the following.

- **Identifying similarities and differences:** Fosters more complex thinking through comparison, contrast, and analysis

- **Summarizing and note taking:** Promotes comprehension through analysis, interpretation, and learner language

- **Reinforcing effort and providing recognition:** Supports perseverance and establishes the connection between effort and success

- **Assigning homework and practice:** Cultivates extended learning beyond the classroom that is directly tied to learning from the classroom

- **Nurturing nonlinguistic representations:** Nurtures cognitive capacity and supports academic growth in second language learners

- **Furthering cooperative learning:** Furthers all learning experiences through social interaction, collaborative thinking, and accountability

- **Setting objectives and providing feedback:** Engenders student accountability, awareness of learning purposes and outcomes, and opportunities for formative feedback

- **Generating and testing hypotheses:** Supports inductive and deductive reasoning as well as critical thinking in all subjects

- **Frames cues, questions, and advance organizers:** Frames learning with visual cues and opportunities for critical consideration and reflection

This list of strategies was not meant to be a simple linear checklist of surface-level instructional strategies. Rather, it was intended as a tool for the reflective practice of teachers and as part of a comprehensive framework of instruction (Marzano, Norford, Paynter, Pickering, & Gaddy, 2001). It guided teachers of all grade levels through the thought processes of effective pedagogy and instructional planning. As a critical first step toward a research-based framework of instruction, these strategies governed the shift toward practices that changed the face of instruction in Lindsay. By implementing these strategies, teachers developed more robust and effective instructional skillsets. In addition, teachers challenged their own long-standing notions of educational practices and worked to shift instructional focus from activities to learning outcomes (Marzano, Norford, et al., 2001). This early focus on instruction in Lindsay Unified was the first time that the district had established a moral imperative for teaching and learning, and it eventually led to the deeper transformation to personalized learning.

The Road Ahead

By the 2004–2005 school year, the success of the district's early improvement efforts was evident in significant increases in the API scores for most of its schools (California Department of Education, 2006). This rise in achievement sparked community pride and inspired more staff members to commit to the district's effort to improve learning. The new chief business officer helped the district function with more solvency while state and local funding allowed for the renovation of school facilities. At the same time, the school board established priorities that helped it operate with more focus, and the renewed spirit of community and inclusion inclined the district and the teachers' union to cooperate. Lindsay Unified hired many new teachers, principals, and district leaders—all of whom expressed and subsequently demonstrated commitment to the district's emerging learner-centered educational philosophy.

This important progress notwithstanding, the district knew that more work was needed. Graduation rates remained low, and dropout rates were still at unacceptable levels. Less than 20 percent of graduates were going on to a four-year college or university and, of those who did, a high number were required to take remedial courses. In addition, gang involvement, teen alcohol and drug use, and teen pregnancy continued to pose challenges within Lindsay Unified schools.

The district leadership team (consisting of the superintendent and the five members of the district's board of trustees) began to realize that by failing to address these chronic issues, the district itself was part of the problem. The system was failing its students by not engaging them or preparing them to succeed in an evolving and highly demanding global society (Fadel, Bialik, & Trilling, 2015). At leadership meetings and in hallway conversations, the team began envisioning deeper systemic transformation. With its cohesion as a foundation, the district leadership team began meeting with consultants to explore how to implement 21st century learning concepts such as collaboration, critical thinking, communication, and creativity as an integral part of the district's framework for instruction. District leadership and staff engaged in these discussions to clarify what these skills were and how to best implement them so that all students would develop these crucial abilities (Bellanca & Brandt, 2010).

In particular, consultant Bea McGarvey met with the members of the Lindsay Unified leadership team over a period of eight months, helping the team develop a future-focused mindset. This mindset included a focus on creating lifelong learners, advancing socioemotional learning, and preparing graduates for an ever-changing society. In short, the leadership team began to envision a future for Lindsay that at one time seemed inconceivable. That work established a foundation that prepared the team to lead the community in developing a strategic design for transforming education—a vision for the district that all stakeholders would ultimately embrace. This strategic direction focused on *personalized learning*—that is, the concept of meeting learners at their actual levels of knowledge and skill so they can reach their fullest academic and personal potential. The road to achieving this vision had not yet been engineered, but this early work set the stage for a new paradigm for the delivery of education in Lindsay schools.

The Strategic Design Process

Early on, district administration came to realize the importance of developing a future-focused strategic design—a document that provided clear direction for the district's ongoing transformation (Schwahn & McGarvey, 2011). The strategic design became the district's blueprint for building and sustaining Lindsay's Performance Based System that resulted in personalized learning.

The board of trustees was fully committed to the newly created strategic design, and its members saw the design as a guide for moving toward what they wanted for all Lindsay learners: greater success, more opportunity, and a better life. Board members had been frustrated with the district's improving—but still poor—achievement results, and they had the courage to identify the problems and push toward a learner-centered system. This commitment was not sparked spontaneously. District leaders, including the superintendent and pivotal district personnel, developed and nurtured the board members' commitment to the new strategic design. A future-focused consultant, Charles

Schwahn, worked closely with the board to help them understand the future that Lindsay graduates would face. The board's priorities began to align more with this future-focused vision. Most importantly, board members recognized and owned their responsibilities as trustees of the learners, not just board members. As trustees, they were willing to grow and learn strategies for effective governance, to be informed, and to set policy, while at the same time empowering and trusting the superintendent and other district staff to run the district without the board micromanaging the process. Initially, the board received professional development aimed at helping members understand the future of education, and they developed leadership capacity to advocate for the Performance Based System. Throughout the transformational process, district leaders worked closely with trustees to ensure that, during uncertain times and periods of ambiguity, the trustees understood their role in helping to realize the vision as well as their responsibility to let district leaders and staff do their jobs. The board was able to remain committed during these early stages of transformation because of strong governing norms that prioritized the needs of learners over politically driven decisions.

District leadership staff played an essential role in building a culture of empowerment and accountability. They decided to avoid top-down edicts about reform and to instead collaboratively engage the community in the process of transformation. In May 2007, the district invited roughly 150 stakeholders to participate in an intensive two-day community work session. As a group, invitees represented the collective voice of the Lindsay Unified community; district leadership, board trustees, principals, teachers, parents (both Spanish and English speaking), support staff, city leaders, and other community members all took part. The group engaged in a series of discussions structured around five core questions.

1. Why do we exist as an organization?
2. What are the core values that will govern how we will interact with one another?

3. What are our guiding principles that will inform our decision making around teaching, learning, learners, and community?

4. What is our vision for the future related to learning, curricula, instruction, assessment, technology, personnel, leadership, and stakeholders?

5. What is the description of our graduates? What do they need to know, be able to do, and be like to lead successful lives when they graduate?

Small groups engaged with these questions and the difficult conversations they engendered. Each group's stakeholders shared personal experiences and suggestions that supported the development of a new model for their community's learners. By the end of the first meeting, the walls were covered with chart paper bearing the thoughts and dreams of the stakeholders. They had clearly expressed their ideas about what the district needed to believe in and work toward in order to prepare Lindsay learners for their futures. As group members brainstormed ideas, established priorities, and explored important concepts, the concepts of *empowering* and *motivating* rose to the top of the list. Collectively, the group agreed on a new district mission statement, which was then formally adopted by the board of trustees on May 21, 2007: Empowering and Motivating for Today and Tomorrow.

Additionally, the group articulated core values, guiding principles, and a new vision for the future. The core values govern professional behavior and how staff work together.

1. Integrity

2. Commitment

3. Excellence

4. Risk taking

5. Teamwork

6. Accountability

7. Improvement

8. Openness

9. Alignment

10. Courage

These ten values are reflective tools that promote continuous improvement and the development of a growth mindset. The ten core values guide leadership in Lindsay and serve as a tool for coaching and supervision.

The guiding principles establish the philosophical outcomes that drive all district work. They center on three categories:

1. Learners and learning

2. Learning facilitators and teaching

3. Learning communities

Within each category, the group articulated the overarching convictions that would guide transformation in the classroom and at each school site. For example, these convictions include "All learners can learn" and "Teaching reflects the current research on learning and cognition." Collectively, these guiding principles served as the framework for more strategic visions.

The vision statements expound upon the guiding principles by focusing on specific elements of the system. The group selected eight components of education for which to define vision statements:

1. Learning

2. Curriculum

3. Instruction

4. Assessment

5. Technology

6. Personnel

7. Leadership

8. Stakeholders

Each vision statement centers on a statement of purpose and is expressed as a definitive, attainable goal. The culminating aspect of Lindsay's version is for its graduates; this is encompassed by the lifelong learning standards, a critical part of the district curriculum. These standards, described in more detail in chapter 2, outline the seven spheres of living that ensure Lindsay graduates will thrive in their college and career prospects, having successfully mastered these competencies.

These various vision-related statements were synthesized into a draft document that was shared with participants for feedback. The district incorporated participants' comments, and, after a series of revisions, the document was formally adopted by the board of trustees in July 2007. Lindsay Unified now had a strategic design that would become both the blueprint and the mandate for the move to the Performance Based System. The strategic design continues to serve as the district's central visioning tool, informing decisions and guiding actions in every aspect of the ongoing transformation.

A Brighter Future for Lindsay Learners

Before the district shifted its system of teaching and learning, Lindsay students were part of an inflexible system that lacked customization and could not respond to the organic nature of learning or the needs of students. As a system, it functioned from a basis of conformity rather than personalization. Imagine a typical fifth-grade class in a traditional time-based system, where every November all students read *The Secret Garden* by Francis Hodgson Burnett. Like most fifth-grade classes, this one has several struggling readers. Although these learners are not yet proficient enough to read *The Secret Garden*, the teacher in this traditional time-based system essentially has to say, "You're in fifth grade now and it's November, so you have to read this book." These students gamely begin, but as they struggle to comprehend what they are reading, they become frustrated. They stop reading and completing the related assignments. Because they can't keep up with their peers, they feel left behind and abandoned by their teacher.

That same fifth-grade class also includes a few students whose reading abilities far outpace the average. One girl, who reads at an eleventh-grade level, read *The Secret Garden* on her own in second grade and is now completely bored with the class. Even so, the teacher expects her to do the same assignments everyone else is doing. Like her peers who struggle with reading—but for very different reasons—this student quickly becomes frustrated with school and disengages from classroom learning activities.

This hypothetical classroom illustrates how school systems that are characterized by time-based structures—such as grade levels, semesters, and 180-day school years—can keep learners from reaching their fullest potential. In a traditional school system, time—not learning—determines students' placement and the curriculum they receive. Students are grouped based on age and all move through the system at the same pace, despite the fact that they do not learn at the same pace. Systems of this nature create large variances in how much each student learns and often fail to engage students because they are treated as compliant consumers of content delivered by teachers.

Lindsay Unified recognized that the time-based system did not serve the needs of its 21st century students. The traditional education system and all of its policies and practices made sense in the past when the goal was merely to sort out the talented from the untalented; those who didn't make the cut could find employment in the fields and factories and focus on earning enough to support a family. Now, education systems are responsible for preparing all students to succeed in an increasingly dynamic and complex world. With this in mind, Lindsay Unified made the decision that students—not time—should be at the center of the education system. Making this shift required a full-scale, districtwide transformation that entailed dismantling the Industrial Age time-based system and replacing it with a personalized, learner-centered system. To reflect that shift, and to serve as a reminder of its importance, the district adopted new terminology for the key players in its education system. In Lindsay Unified, students are referred to as *learners*; teachers are viewed as *learning facilitators* rather than as deliverers of content; and together they turn schools into *learning communities* (Schwahn & McGarvey, 2011). This shift in language is further explained in chapter 2.

Lindsay Unified's new approach is known as the Performance Based System—that is, a system in which the culture, learning, pacing, and other aspects of instruction are personalized to meet learner needs and ensure all learners learn. A fundamental aspect of this system is that, rather than moving ahead and receiving assignments based on what grade or semester they are in, learners progress through clearly defined learning outcomes only as they are able to demonstrate mastery of those learning targets. Lindsay Unified's system is also distinguished by its focus on learners' empowerment and ownership of learning. Learner agency, a core component of this model, fosters a culture of shared responsibility, advocacy, and transparency in which learners and learning facilitators co-construct learning and assessment. This agency begins with the shared vision and norms of the learning environment and extends to the learning experiences. Learning experiences are structured by the needs of the learners and include formative feedback between the learning facilitator and learner to ensure a path to rigorous learning and mastery of content. The Performance Based System removes the arbitrary structures of its predecessor such as seat time as an equation of learning, point values for assignments, and teacher-centered classrooms in which the teacher is the keeper of the knowledge.

The variety of speeds at which learners move through the curriculum is addressed through a structure that allows for grouping and regrouping of learners at any point in the learning process, regardless of the time of the year (Schwahn & McGarvey, 2014). Unlike tracking (which traditionally places learners on a fixed path based on prior performance or perceived abilities), the Performance Based System allows for fluidity in the learning process. Because learners are grouped by what they're currently working on, not by traditional grade level, they work in mixed-age groupings on specific content or skills. For example, a ten-year-old learner who is reading at a third-grade level but doing sixth-grade mathematics would be grouped for each content area with learners of various ages who are performing at roughly the same level. These grouping structures, in addition to allowing for more focused instruction and opportunities for acceleration, support a more collaborative and cooperative learning experience for all learners. For many learners, these grouping structures help to enhance self-efficacy, personal empowerment, and intrinsic motivation.

In Lindsay Unified's Performance Based System, learning is the constant and time is the variable. Because time is flexible, the district can meet and engage all learners at their respective levels to ensure that everyone learns. Lindsay Unified has implemented four foundational concepts in its Performance Based System. Together, these concepts have brought about a dramatic shift in the learning paradigm, leading to greater academic and personal success for learners. The foundational concepts are as follows.

- Personalized mastery
- Rigorous learning
- Transparency and shared accountability
- Learners' ownership of their education

These concepts are described in the following sections.

Personalized Mastery

To shift to the Performance Based System, all adults in the Lindsay Unified School District and the larger community had to commit to a new vision for Lindsay learners. Most important, they had to embrace the belief that learners learn in different ways and in different time frames and therefore need personalized learning experiences to ensure their success. Putting this new vision of a personalized learning experience into action meant leaving behind the one-size-fits-all curriculum and adding a focus on the development of the socioemotional skills that are needed for personal success. Learners are now valued as individuals with different interests, aspirations, learning styles, motivations, and learning needs—all factors that inform and guide learning facilitators in personalizing instruction, including what, how, and when each one will learn and how he or she will demonstrate mastery.

Transformed structures allow learners to advance only when they are able to demonstrate mastery of the required course material. Implementation requires an assessment system that is aligned with the curriculum, is completely integrated into instruction, and features performance tasks through which learners can demonstrate proficiency. Ultimately, the system's focus is on results and accountability. By maintaining high expectations for every Lindsay learner, personalizing the instruction, and ensuring that assessments allow learners to demonstrate learning in a variety of ways, the Performance Based System ensures that learners have equitable opportunities to achieve. Personal engagement in learning, with the encouragement of invested adults, helps Lindsay learners develop a greater sense of self-efficacy to pursue their lifelong goals. When learners are self-directed and autonomous, they are truly motivated and empowered to learn.

Rigorous Learning

The second central concept is rigorous learning. Lindsay Unified's Performance Based System is grounded in a set of rigorous standards drawn from the California State Standards and the Common Core State Standards and organized by the district into units of study referred to as *measurement topics*. These measurement topics, comprised of multiple standards with related learning outcomes, encompass the knowledge and skills that Lindsay learners must develop as they move through their education. Using the measurement topics as a starting point, the district crafted a high-quality curriculum that clearly communicates what learners will learn and how they will demonstrate that they have mastered the content. Along with academic content, this curriculum includes 21st century and lifelong learning skills that the district recognizes as essential for college, career, and personal success.

Lindsay Unified's curriculum is both guaranteed and viable. *Guaranteed* means that all learners will master the competencies contained within the identified curriculum. *Viable* means that the curriculum focuses only on the essential learning outcomes such that there is enough time available to address all topics identified in the curriculum. Instead of covering standards in a cursory manner as is often the case in traditional curricula, a guaranteed and viable curriculum ensures learners grasp the content in depth. In addition, all increased instructional and learning time is used to achieve mastery.

Because mastery is required, the district has consistently increased the academic rigor of the learners' school experiences. The first shifts in rigor began with the implementation of 21st century skills, such as critical thinking and creativity, as well as the use of strategies from *Classroom Instruction That Works* (Marzano, Pickering, & Pollock, 2001) as part of the instructional framework. With these tools, learning facilitators created more challenging learning experiences. Learning goals and the associated rubrics that define mastery became the core of the learning process.

The guaranteed and viable curriculum also requires that learners produce evidence of mastery for every measurement topic. In a traditional system, students are typically promoted as long as their grades across the course average out to a passing grade. This results in many students learning only some of the information. Through its guaranteed and viable curriculum, Lindsay Unified promises the community that its graduates will have mastered essential, transferrable learning that prepares them for lives beyond the classroom.

Transparency and Shared Accountability

Because performance-based models are built on the idea that learners progress only when they have demonstrated mastery, transparency regarding content and expectations is essential, as is shared accountability for advancing learning. To ensure transparency, Lindsay Unified has developed clear, explicit learning goals with comprehensive and aligned assessments. To engender shared accountability, the district has taken steps to ensure that learner results are clearly understood by key stakeholders.

Learners must know exactly what is expected of them in terms of the content and skills that they are to learn through each learning progression. They also must understand the criteria for demonstrating mastery of the related standards. In a time-based system, a learner who has not gained the expected knowledge or skill might receive a D and still move to the next grade level. In contrast, in a performance-based model, learners are required to demonstrate mastery before progressing to the next level of learning, and thus are held accountable to the curriculum and assessments. When learners clearly understand where they are in the progression of learning, they become empowered, self-directed, and personally accountable for their learning.

At the classroom level, learning facilitators center instruction on the learning targets and translate them into learning goals that are tracked by learners and their families. The role of learning goals is to foster more authentic learning, developmentally aligned instruction, and learner accountability (Marzano, 2009). For example, learners who need to master a reading fluency learning target will use the learning target to analyze their current reading capacity, consider what proficiency means, and set goals to achieve mastery. Their learning facilitator might track their progress in multiple ways that ensure transparency and accountability, such as individual progress documents, a class reading progress chart, scores in the district's learning management system, or conversations with their families. At a site level, learning directors and principals monitor learners' various levels of progress on all learning targets and support communication of these targets and learners' progress to families and the district. In the Performance Based System, the teacher's gradebook is no longer hidden from learners. Instead, all measures of learning are consistently available and used by all stakeholders in support of growth and mastery.

To develop shared accountability for learning, learners and all key stakeholders need real-time access to assessment results. Toward this goal, Lindsay Unified engaged in the development of a web-based learning management system (LMS), currently known as Empower. The Empower platform handles all aspects of the learning process: delivering and managing instructional content; identifying and assessing individual learning; tracking progress toward learning goals; and collecting and presenting data and results. Through this system, learners and parents can view assessment results, track progress, and monitor personalized learning plans. Learning facilitators can access learner data to track performance on district benchmarks and classroom assessments, which, in turn, informs instructional decisions. Finally, systemwide data generated by Empower provide feedback that key stakeholders can use in efforts to continuously improve the Performance Based System. With such transparency and access, learners benefit from the development of an intrinsic motivation that supports goal attainment.

No longer does the responsibility fall to one entity within the school to communicate a learner's progress. Instead, there is a web of stakeholders who are empowered to hold each other accountable for the sake of learners and advocate for what best serves learners' needs. Learners can check on their progress daily and hold discussions with both peers and learning facilitators, which enables learning facilitators to recognize learners' needs and communicate those needs to parents, site administrators, and relevant instructional support personnel. Parents no longer have to wait for report cards to ensure their learners are making progress and can engage in discussions with site personnel at any time. Accountability to learning is also reinforced through district data analysis sessions that involve site principals and key site instructional leads.

Learners' Ownership of Their Education

One of the most powerful differences between performance- and time-based education systems is the learner's role. Because Lindsay's Performance Based System is driven by the needs and decisions of the learners themselves, each learner is an active participant in the education process. Historically, public education systems have viewed learners—whether explicitly or implicitly—as incapable of making important decisions regarding their education, but Lindsay Unified believes that learners can and should control their own learning.

This vision is made real by the district's learner-centered instructional model, which shifts traditional student-teacher roles. In Lindsay Unified, the adults guide the learning with clear objectives, but learners have legitimate voice and choice. Teachers serve as learning facilitators who collaborate with learners to guide and support them. As learning facilitators, they mentor learners in setting personal goals, determining appropriate pace, and selecting relevant learning activities and assessments, all of which increase learners' ownership of the learning process. Ultimately, it is the learners who take responsibility for completing activities and demonstrating proficiency. This process is customizable and flexible so that learners may accelerate in areas of strength and adopt a more deliberate pace in areas they find more challenging.

To support learners' ownership of their learning, Lindsay Unified has made technology a central tool in the Performance Based System. All learners have access to the technology that they need to engage in self-directed learning, collaborate with the global community, and explore personal interests. While technology is one important component of the education experience, it is the focus on learner agency that drives the district's Performance Based System. The system is truly learner centered, not technology centered.

Summary

Lindsay Unified, like many districts across the nation, had been troubled by a long history of low academic achievement by its learners. Among the challenges it faced in trying to improve learner outcomes was how to meet the needs of its increasingly diverse population. Leaders at Lindsay Unified recognized that traditional attempts at reform, such as isolated curricular initiatives, professional development workshops, and other piecemeal changes, would be insufficient. Changing the system to meet the needs of learners would require the district to move beyond isolated reform activities to a complete and systemic transformation of education.

Lindsay's Performance Based System addresses these challenges in a systemic fashion with a framework that prioritizes learners. It safeguards against the pitfalls of a traditional educational model by ensuring personalized learning and mastery. Learners are cognitively and instructionally challenged as they move through a strategic curriculum at a pace that is customized to their needs and styles. Learning targets and outcomes are transparent and can be accessed by all stakeholders. Learning facilitators, site and district administrators, and parents work collaboratively to consider a learner's progress and make informed decisions to provide instructional support. With more voices in the discussion, learners and stakeholders share responsibility and work together for solutions and continued growth.

During the preliminary stages of change, Lindsay Unified focused on the following areas.

- Addressing immediate business and organizational issues
- Building leadership capacity
- Building harmonious relationships with staff
- Ensuring that the board of trustees understands and supports the reform efforts

- Improving instructional practices
- Seeking out research-based practices and outside perspectives
- Engaging key stakeholders in jointly developing a strategic design

Karly

As a learner in Lindsay Unified's Performance Based System, Karly began high school with personal goals to guide her future beyond graduation. She had always enjoyed science and knew she wanted to attend college to study either biology or physics. She looked forward to classes each day because they were relevant and authentic and meant to prepare her for postsecondary life. Coming from a home that lacked educational experience, her learning facilitators were essential in ensuring she understood her learning progression, what mastery looked like, and how to apply it rigorously. While her father could not help her academically, he supported her learning and trusted the new system to help Karly with her goals. By the end of freshman year, Karly was working on advanced content—the kind that in a traditional model would have only been available to her in eleventh grade. She graduated from Lindsay High School at the end of what would have been her junior year and enrolled at University of California, Irvine the following year to major in physics. Because Lindsay's Performance Based System is designed to allow learners to move at an accelerated pace through a guaranteed and viable curriculum, Karly had access to a personalized route to college and career readiness.

CHAPTER 2

Creating a New Culture

Lindsay Unified Core Values

- INTEGRITY: The embodiment of honesty, fairness, trustworthiness, honor, and consistent adherence to high-level moral principles

- COMMITMENT: A willingness to devote full energies and talents to the successful completion of undertakings

- EXCELLENCE: A desire for, and pursuit of, the highest quality in any undertaking, process, product, or result

- RISK TAKING: Taking initiative, innovating, breaking the mold, and speaking out in sincere attempts to support core values

- TEAMWORK: Working collaboratively and cooperatively toward achieving a common recognized end

- ACCOUNTABILITY: Taking responsibility for the content and process of decisions made, actions taken, and the resulting outcomes

- IMPROVEMENT: A commitment to continuously enhance the quality of personal and organizational results, performances, and processes

continued →

- OPENNESS: A willingness and desire to receive, consider, and act ethically on information and possibilities of all kinds
- ALIGNMENT: The purposeful, direct matching of decisions, resources, and organizational structures with the organization's vision
- COURAGE: The willingness of individuals and organizations to risk themselves despite the likelihood of negative consequences or fear

Source: Lindsay Unified School District, 2007.

Moving an education system's primary focus from time to learning requires not only practical changes but also a cultural shift in the essential behaviors, dispositions, and orientations of district leadership, learning facilitators, and the learners themselves. To guide the overall cultural shift and facilitate Lindsay Unified's transition to the Performance Based System, the district's leadership team agreed on a set of core values. The team members identified the values they thought should undergird the work of everyone in the district, define how people interact with each other, and inform which strategies are employed to fulfill the mission. The core values are the essential tenets of the way things are done in Lindsay. They became the moral code of professional behavior that is now the norm for staff members in Lindsay Unified. These norms, however, grew out of the collective process that developed the strategic design, which includes the foundational beliefs and guiding principles.

Major shifts in mindset were also a large part of transitioning to Lindsay's Performance Based System. The district moved its collective mindset from covering content with a time-based emphasis to focusing on learner performance and learning for mastery. A focus on lifelong learning, rather than a focus on learning for the time being, leads to higher student success, both in school and later on in life.

Foundational Beliefs and Guiding Principles

Transitioning to a learner-centered culture required Lindsay Unified's learning community to establish and collectively agree on meaningful guiding principles that clearly align to the district's mission and vision. As complex decisions are made, these guiding principles are referenced to ensure that decisions align with the collective beliefs of the community. Failure to have or to follow such principles would make the transition to performance-based education nearly impossible. These principles establish a uniform direction that guides all district work, from the purchase of new curriculum materials to the hiring of learning facilitators. Every decision is measured against the guiding principles to determine how it will advance or detract from the district's vision. The beliefs and guiding principles function as an anchor for the development of the Performance Based System.

When drafting the guiding principles, the district started from three foundational beliefs about learners.

1. All learners can learn.

2. Learners acquire knowledge in different ways and time frames.

3. Successful learning breeds continued success, which influences esteem, attitude, and motivation.

Recognizing that learning facilitators are the single most important factor in learners' academic achievement (Marzano, 2012; Marzano, Pickering, & Pollock, 2001), the district next identified three guiding principles for its learning facilitators.

1. Learning facilitators are models of continuous learning and improvement; they inspire, motivate, and empower learners.

2. Learning facilitators set the conditions for a safe, welcoming, and joyful classroom environment. They relate to and connect with learners.

3. Learning facilitators are knowledgeable and competent in pedagogy and human development, which enables them

to design personalized instruction to meet learners at their developmental levels.

In addition, Lindsay Unified developed guiding principles for the learning community, including both the school community and the broader Lindsay community. The most basic of these principles is that all stakeholders in the community are partners in educating Lindsay's learners. People in Lindsay work together to ensure communal understanding of and belief in the mission and vision of the district, they invest in and support it, and they recognize that the school system is the heart of the community. Learning facilitators and all other adults must hold high expectations for all learners and provide highly engaging, well-supported, personalized learning experiences that fit their needs.

Finally, the district identified six guiding principles that capture the district's convictions about learning.

1. Mistakes are inherent in the learning process.
2. Learning and curiosity are basic human drives.
3. Learners require positive and validating relationships with learning facilitators.
4. Learning is enhanced by meaningful, real-life experiences requiring complex thinking.
5. Learning is fun.
6. Learning is fostered by frequent formative feedback.

Additionally, learning should be future focused. Future-focused learning recognizes that the world learners will live in is still unfolding and thus demands that educators modify and design experiences that will prepare learners for success in an unknown world.

Collectively, the guiding principles send the message that learning is not the same as "doing school." Rather, it is a dynamic, natural experience that should be engaging for learners. In the broadest sense, human beings are wired to be curious lifelong learners. The guiding principles redirect the attention of the Lindsay community to the true nature of learning.

Adoption of a Visionary Vocabulary

One of the first steps in changing the district culture was to change the ways that Lindsay learners, learning facilitators, staff, and community members spoke about education. Language is at the core of cultural perceptions of schooling. Words paint a particular mental picture, which, in turn, affects the actions that people take.

The district leadership team worked closely with a consultant, Chuck Schwahn, to choose new vocabulary designed to evoke new mental images related to education. A set of exercises presented familiar words—such as *student, teacher,* and *school*—and asked team members to describe the images that these words brought to mind. The word *teacher* typically calls to mind an adult standing in front of a class, delivering a prepared lecture, while *student* prompts the image of a child sitting at a desk, receiving instruction. The team members collectively recognized that this language suggested images of traditional education that did not align with the emerging Lindsay Unified vision.

The leadership team then focused on describing what students, teachers, and schools would look like in the vision they had for Lindsay Unified. From these descriptions, team members generated a new, visionary vocabulary that moved the focus from teaching to learning. By deliberately introducing different terms—such as *learners* and *learning facilitators*—Lindsay Unified intended to disrupt those traditional mental images of what goes on in a classroom and create new ones. The following terms were instrumental in the cultural shift.

- *Learners:*
  - Formerly called *students*
  - No longer passive recipients
  - Become active participants, constructors of knowledge, and authors of their own education experiences
- *Learning facilitators:*
  - Formerly called *teachers*
  - Facilitate learning experiences
  - Co-construct understandings alongside learners

- *Learning environments:*
  - Formerly called *classrooms*
  - Places where learning experiences occur
  - Can encompass a classroom, a laboratory, or any other setting in which learning happens
- *Learning communities:*
  - A group of stakeholders
  - Can encompass one school, the whole district, and anyone involved in the learning process
- *Learning outcomes:*
  - Defined expectations organized in a progression that can be comprised of single or multiple learning targets
- *Learning target:*
  - The understanding or skills from the standards that help form learning outcomes and articulate what the learner would need to show mastery

The leadership team recognized that changing deeply embedded words like *teacher* and *student* would be a tremendous challenge. It approached the shift in two ways. First, each member of the district leadership team and school-site leadership teams personally committed to using the new vocabulary in his or her oral and written language. Second, the district leadership team presented the new vocabulary to each of the learning communities. These presentations engaged all members of the learning community in the same visualization exercises that the leadership team had initially completed, helping stakeholders across the district understand the philosophical underpinnings of the new terminology. These presentations raised awareness of the role that the new vocabulary would play in achieving Lindsay Unified's transformative vision, but this was only an introduction. The more substantial work occurred at the learning-community level and was consistently reinforced by principals, all of whom had committed to modeling the new language and holding the learning facilitators at their sites accountable for using the new vocabulary. While challenging, adopting new terminology reinforced the vision and served as a constant reminder of the deep cultural change the district was engaged in.

A Mastery Mindset for a Results-Driven Culture

Another major shift in culture was moving the district's collective mindset from covering content in accordance with time-based pacing guides to facilitating learning for mastery, with its inherent focus on learner performance. Each day, learners are engaged at their developmental learning levels and are challenged to demonstrate the results of their learning experiences. They cannot progress to the next level in a content area until they have successfully demonstrated understanding or skill in a required proficiency. With this shift, it was made clear to learners, learning facilitators, and the broader community that the district would no longer award barely passing grades so learners could move forward without having mastered the required content or skills, nor would the district advance learners based on compliance, good behavior, or seat time.

In the traditional time-based system, both teachers and students operate under the status quo of social promotion and grade averaging. If an eighth-grade student cannot read at grade level and has not passed most classes, he or she may still be promoted to high school, further expanding the academic gaps that undermine college and career readiness. Likewise, in a traditional classroom, students work to accumulate points toward an averaged grade that usually includes a cumulative final exam. Their grades can also include points for good behavior, extra credit, and other factors that have little to do with what they actually learned. In the Performance Based System, however, learners must demonstrate academic proficiency to progress, ensuring that academic gaps are addressed and learners enter each content level prepared for the next progression of rigor and application.

Lindsay Unified's vision of personalized mastery learning emphasizes results and paces instruction according to learners' individual needs, rather than basing it on content that must be covered. In a traditional system, the pace is often defined by the number of instructional units the teacher must teach in a year. If the teacher can only allot two weeks to a particular unit, he or she must move on to the next unit at the end of that time, regardless of whether the students have learned the content. In the Performance Based System, learners take as much or as little time as they need to learn the content and then move on when they are ready. This vision is reinforced with a curriculum that clearly defines learner *outcomes*—what learners must know and be able to do—grounded in rigorous, authentic tasks that require critical thinking, problem solving, and communication skills.

The *mastery mindset* means that all efforts are focused on helping learners master required content and skills and demonstrate that proficiency. A significant part of the learning facilitator's role is to skillfully integrate multiple opportunities for learners to demonstrate mastery into their lessons through the use of formative assessment, digital learning tools, performance-based assessment, presentations, and peer-to-peer instruction. By offering varied opportunities for learners to show mastery of what is being studied, learning facilitators are better able to meet the needs of diverse learners and more completely and accurately measure learner achievement.

A results-driven culture depends on high-quality data on learner progress being readily available to both learners and learning facilitators. Learners—the primary stakeholders in a data-driven culture such as the Performance Based System—are involved in gathering evidence and monitoring progress, which heightens their ownership in the learning process. To that end, Lindsay Unified adopted a web-based learning management system (LMS) called Educate (later Empower), which provides access to data on specific learning targets directly aligned to the California State Standards. Learners use the LMS to access their own learning results, track their progress, and make decisions regarding their personalized mastery plans. Learning facilitators also use the LMS to track learner performance, and then use the data to improve instruction. The insistence on mastery and proof of that mastery is central to the Performance Based System.

Focus on Lifelong Learning

Finally, district leaders asked themselves, "What kind of human being is the Lindsay Unified graduate?" It was clear, through the course of the strategic design's development, that the ideal graduate was one with well-developed socioemotional skills that could be harnessed for personal, academic, and socioeconomic advancement. The district and its stakeholders wanted graduates who are lifelong learners—self-motivated to pursue knowledge and seek out experiences that expand their worldviews. In determining what traits would constitute lifelong learning, stakeholders focused on categories that would support academic initiatives and the development of the grit, mindset, and perseverance learners need for successful, productive adulthood.

Ultimately, seven socioemotional competencies (or *spheres of living*) were identified. These spheres work in tandem to support the development of the whole learner.

1. **A well-balanced person (personal sphere):** A graduate who can use goal setting, feedback, and a guiding set of beliefs to create a balanced lifestyle and respond to changes and adversity

2. **A self-directed, lifelong learner (learning sphere):** A graduate who possesses and evaluates core knowledge, demonstrates the habits of continuous improvement, and self-assesses his or her own learning and progress

3. **A caring, compassionate person (relationships sphere):** A graduate who uses interpersonal skills, empathy, and problem-solving skills to develop an awareness and understanding of other people and their perspectives

4. **A civic-minded person (civic sphere):** A graduate who engages with various levels of civic issues, contributes to community endeavors, and recognizes the history and principles of democratic citizenship

5. **A responsible global citizen (global sphere):** A graduate who responds locally to global environmental issues,

endeavors to protect human rights worldwide, and communicates the complexities of such issues from differing points of view

6. **A quality producer and resource manager (economic sphere):** A graduate who, through a positive attitude and work ethic of continuous improvement, adapts to rapidly changing work environments including new technologies, resource management, and quality standards

7. **A culturally aware person (cultural sphere):** A graduate who values the arts, other cultures, diversity, and the heritage associated with them; who can engage others without cultural stereotyping; and who demonstrates individual responsibility with an emphasis on empathy, nurturing, and cooperation

In the development of its Performance Based System, Lindsay Unified emphasized that the person a learner becomes as an adult is more important than the academic content he or she learns. These competencies emerged as the Lindsay Unified lifelong learning standards, which are discussed in further detail in chapter 5.

Summary

In the desire to reform district culture, stakeholders in Lindsay could not merely renovate the existing one. Instead, through strategic shifts and results-driven thinking, it constructed a new culture based on essential behaviors, dispositions, and orientations. The guiding beliefs and principles provided a new moral imperative for staff and stakeholders. By adopting a visionary vocabulary, the district changed deeply ingrained conceptions of teaching and learning. With a focus on mastery and results, the district shifted its orientation to one of transparency, accountability, and achievement. By envisioning the lifelong learning capacity of its graduates, the district envisioned a school system that stakeholders could consider their own. These cultural changes formed the foundation for continued transformation.

For Lindsay Unified, creating a new culture as a foundation for personalized learning involved the following steps.

- Developing a set of core values
- Establishing guiding principles and beliefs
- Enacting a visionary vocabulary
- Adopting a mastery mindset
- Defining the ideal graduate
- Identifying socioemotional competencies for graduates

Omar

In his years in Lindsay Unified, Omar, an English learner, always struggled with his English language arts classes. In particular, he felt he never knew what was expected of him in his writing and speaking. When Lindsay transformed to the Performance Based System, he began to gain clarity about what he needed to learn and what proficiency looked like. While working on an oral presentation for his project on immigration, Omar admitted to his learning facilitator that he had always been nervous speaking in front of others because of his English skills. His learning facilitator suggested they use the presentation as an opportunity to work on public speaking and practice some lifelong learning skills as well, including goal setting, feedback, and responding to difficult situations. After working with his learning facilitator to understand the rubric for oral presentations and examining some exemplars, Omar practiced in front of his peers. They gave him feedback on his verbal and nonverbal skills and helped him develop a presentation that addressed aspects of proficiency on the rubric. On the day of his presentation, despite his nerves, Omar delivered a proficient presentation. In the reflective discussion with his learning facilitator later that day, he admitted that he "never knew he could be such a great speaker." Because the Performance Based System was shifting the culture to value clear expectations, formative feedback, and lifelong learning, Omar developed new capacities and confidence in his own learning.

CHAPTER 3

Transforming Leadership

continued →

- District leaders have created an organizational culture that values and rewards learner success, cooperation, innovation, and quality.

- Learning facilitators are also leaders and are recognized as such. They are involved in the critical decisions that impact their own professional lives and the lives of learners.

Source: Lindsay Unified School District, 2007.

Once the vision for a personalized and learner-centered system had been established, the district leadership team recognized its responsibility to communicate this vision and model commitment to it. To do so, they adopted a powerful framework for future-focused leadership (figure 3.1) based on the work of Charles Schwahn and William Spady (2010) in their book *Total Leaders 2.0: Leading in the Age of Empowerment.* According to this framework for future-focused leadership, a strategic design is the key to creating productive change. As described previously, the Lindsay community developed a strategic design comprising a mission statement, core values, and guiding principles. The strategic design also included vision statements for personnel, curricula, assessment, instruction, learning, technology, and stakeholders.

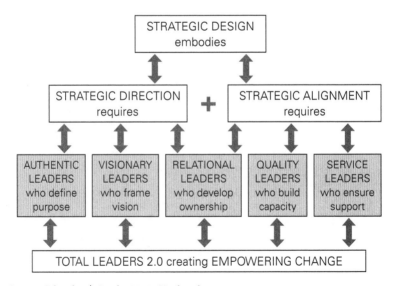

Source: Schwahn & Spady, 2010. Used with permission.

Figure 3.1: Strategic design alignment framework.

Enacting the strategic design requires two lines of action: (1) strategic direction and (2) strategic alignment. *Strategic direction* sets initiatives and defines plans, actions, and goals. It is supported by leaders who are authentic, define purpose, and provide a clearly framed vision. *Strategic alignment* is the practice of ensuring that programs, structures, and decisions are in alignment with the strategic direction. In essence, each component of the organization must be functioning and working in a way that builds cohesiveness. To create strategic alignment, quality leaders focus on building capacity to carry out change, and service-oriented leaders ensure that their personnel have appropriate support. Leaders who focus on developing relationships and collective owner-ship work toward both strategic direction and strategic alignment.

After the formal adoption of the strategic design, Lindsay Unified's leadership team communicated the transformation to the Performance Based System to all stakeholders. This included developing for the Lindsay community presentations that explained the core content and proposed changes in depth. Articulating a clear vision was a top prior-ity, and the team worked especially hard with principals and other site leaders to ensure that these leaders not only were on board with the mission and beliefs, but also that they embraced the new vision and could communicate their own commitment to other staff. As principals began working with site teams to implement the strategic design, the leadership team monitored the implementation closely for alignment with the new vision.

The district leadership team articulated and embraced the vision; however, it knew that the most important work would happen within Lindsay's learning communities. These communities needed to trans-form into the ecosystems that would foster achievement, respond to learner needs, and develop future graduates who would exemplify the vision of Lindsay's Performance Based System. For this reason, empow-ering principals and learning facilitators to be change agents was a top priority. This stemmed from the notion of shared leadership and a bal-ance between the positional capacity of both site and district admin-istration. To ensure that principals had enough autonomy to meet the needs of their learners, they had the responsibility of developing their own site-level budgets. In addition, personnel decisions were to be made at the site level, and principals had the ability to establish schedules and define the roles of learning facilitators and other staff members (with alignment to the strategic design). For example, whereas one learning community might invest its personnel funds in a counselor, another may hire a reading specialist based on learner needs. Although there was flexibility in such decisions, there was oversight to ensure alignment to the district's mission and vision. Learning communities could, within the bounded autonomy provided by the district's strategic design, make decisions that were best for their sites. This created deep investment and empowerment for all leaders as well as a balance between autonomy and system alignment.

As another effort to ensure alignment, all district and site leaders participated in training on the strategic design components related to their respective roles in the new system's restructuring and implementation. Sessions included unpacking the various strategic design components, learning how to teach these components to others, and rehearsing critical conversations that would deepen and defend the commitment to the strategic design. The role of leadership throughout the district shifted well beyond traditional management responsibilities and became one of empowerment and servant leadership toward accomplishing the mission and vision of the learning community.

Transforming leadership in Lindsay Unified is an ongoing process. To continuously improve their leadership practices, principals and other leaders engage in monthly focus sessions dedicated to the development of instructional leadership. Initially, these sessions centered on ensuring clarity and understanding the basics of what a learner-centered environment looks like and how to employ Marzano's (2007) instructional design questions and strategies. For site administrators, it was imperative to impart strategies for building a cohesive team and engaging in collaborative problem solving surrounding the early challenges of transforming the system. From the standpoint of supporting learning facilitators, site administrators learned how to conduct effective walkthroughs, develop feedback protocols, and host strategic alignment conversations. These focus sessions continue to occur on a regular basis.

In addition, every three weeks, leaders engage in a cycle of inquiry to study achievement results of identified learner groups, such as preschool, special education, English learners, or learners from migrant families. As a group, district leaders visit learning communities, conduct learning environment walkthroughs, discuss findings, and debrief with site principals to identify both high-quality elements of instruction and areas for improvement. These identified areas for improvement determine the appropriate focus for professional development. For example, if upon observation, a site's learners are struggling with mathematics instruction, district leaders meet site administrators to brainstorm possible causes, solutions, and necessary supports. These supports could include professional development for learning facilitators, supplementary curricular materials, effective planning strategies, strategic grouping of learners, or other possible solutions. Site leaders create goals to improve any identified areas and, with the support of the district, they continue to develop and monitor their results.

Just as feedback is essential for learners and learning facilitator growth, it is also critical for district and site leaders to receive ongoing information about their performance. A leadership rubric, based on the strategic design alignment framework (see figure 3.1 on page 38; Schwahn & Spady, 2010), guides personal reflection, supervision, and coaching of leaders. Leaders receive feedback with regard to their ability to define purpose, frame vision, develop ownership, build capacity, and ensure support. An important element of leadership development with this framework and rubric is a culture of transparency. This culture ensures supervisors of all levels adhere to a code of candor with the leaders they supervise regarding their leadership style, areas of strength, and areas for growth. The feedback occurs in both formal and informal settings, including dialogue, written reflection, goal setting, and formal evaluations. These feedback loops foster personal and shared accountability around each leader's goals and responsibilities. Such transparent, clear, and goal-driven feedback is essential in any educational transformation effort because if the leaders themselves do not embrace a professional growth mindset, ownership of their own learning and development, and the ability to drive the mission and vision forward, they do a disservice to anyone they lead and perpetuate the ineffective practices of the past.

At various points in the transformation process, it became apparent to the leadership team that challenges to maintaining an effective team and healthy organization still existed. On occasion, relationships were strained or there was a clear lack of trust among key people in leadership positions. To ensure that the mission and vision of Lindsay Unified became a reality, district leadership confronted the challenges to the core culture in a direct and consistent manner. It implemented several strategies to build, support, and sustain a healthy culture. These strategies include extensive work in five focus areas, discussed in the following sections: *The Five Dysfunctions of a Team*, *The Advantage*, core value rubrics, The Breakthrough Coach, and Collaborative Leadership Lindsay.

The Five Dysfunctions of a Team

In 2004, Patrick Lencioni's book *The Five Dysfunctions of a Team* (2002) became an important leadership tool for the district. The district adopted the book's model to evaluate leadership team dynamics, expand strengths, and identify and make improvements in areas of weaknesses. Lencioni's Team Assessment of the Five Dysfunctions, shown in figure 3.2, would serve as an important accelerator for organizational development for almost a decade, until the core value rubrics (discussed in more detail on pages 45–47) became the essential assessment of team dynamics and leadership culture.

The model suggests that truly effective and cohesive teams trust one another, engage in unfiltered conflict around ideas, commit to decisions and plans of action, hold themselves and one another accountable for delivering on those plans, and focus on the achievement of collective results. The model is constructed as a hierarchical pyramid with trust as the base because it is foundational to all relationships. Once team members establish trust in each other, healthy teams are able to engage in constructive conflict. With this foundation, they are committed and fully engaged in the work and can express their positions authentically and establish agreements to hold each other accountable

Source: Lencioni, 2002. Used with permission.

Figure 3.2: Team assessment of the five dysfunctions.

to predetermined standards of performance. Only when a team begins with trust, engages in healthy conflict, commits to all endeavors, and takes ownership of its work can it become results driven.

Based on internal cultural assessments, Lindsay Unified identified weaknesses in each of these areas. Leadership development to address these weaknesses included direct instruction, coaching, and opportunities for reflection by individuals and groups. A significant amount of the monthly district leadership meeting time is focused on the development of cohesive and fully aligned teams. Team-building activities include sharing personal histories, taking personality inventories, engaging in role playing, practicing peer accountability scenarios, and voicing public statements of commitments to excellence. These activities (and many others) serve to create openness and foster trust, which ultimately forge strength and unity in the team.

The Advantage

In July 2012, the leadership team chose to study *The Advantage: Why Organizational Health Trumps Everything Else in Business* (Lencioni, 2012). Building on Lencioni's five dysfunctions model, Lindsay Unified leaders engaged in deep work related to organizational health—focusing particularly on Lencioni's four activities for organizational health (figure 3.3). The team focused on maximizing learner success through the support of healthy teams that are fully aligned with the strategic design, eliminating politics and confusion, and ensuring high degrees of morale and productivity.

Source: Lencioni, 2012. Used with permission.

Figure 3.3: Four activities for organizational health.

A core group of thirteen site and district leaders convened, each of whom had a particular interest, skill, or experience related to organizational development. In July 2014, the group, known as the

Organizational Health (OH) Team, participated in advanced training from Lencioni's consulting group. During the subsequent school year, the OH Team created a customized curriculum related to organizational health for use with identified district-level teams. This curriculum consists of ten modules developed by the core team. The first seven modules, built from the tenets of the five dysfunctions model, focus on the elements and strategies of effective team development. Module eight reinforces the strategic design as the unifying document in the district. In the ninth module, participants are trained on how to embody and communicate the strategic design to others. The closing module inspires participants to recognize, reinforce, and celebrate their role in making the mission and vision of the organization a reality. The OH Team conducts ongoing professional development with various departments to ensure effective team development and sustain alignment to Lindsay Unified's mission and vision. The core team continues to meet regularly to evaluate effectiveness and further develop the next steps in organizational health.

Core Value Rubrics

Lindsay Unified created a strong moral code among all staff by identifying and establishing a common set of core values: integrity, commitment, excellence, risk taking, teamwork, accountability, improvement, openness, alignment, and courage. These core values establish a collective understanding of how staff work and interact. The core values provide common ground and clearly define the expectations for professional behavior and responsibility of all Lindsay Unified staff. More deeply, there is now an expectation that Lindsay Unified leadership and employees represent the district at all times. Core values cannot be turned on and turned off—they represent the moral fiber of each individual.

The core values, established as a key component of the strategic design, describe the behaviors that are needed for district staff to successfully work together and advance Lindsay Unified's mission. After determining the core values, team members collectively designed rubrics that unpack the core values and show what they look like, sound like, and feel like when put into action in the workplace. For each core value, the rubric articulates behaviors, actions, and dispositions in three levels of progression: the Lindsay leader, the passive leader, and the underminer. Although the term *underminer* may appear negative, it does not result in punitive actions but does aim to generate personal reflection. Ingrained in the Lindsay Unified culture is a growth mindset that allows individuals to make mistakes and strive for growth and improvement. The core value rubrics are used as a tool to frame critical and transparent conversations, both proactively and when core values are violated, so individuals and teams can grow as professionals and hold one another accountable. Table 3.1 depicts the core value rubric for integrity.

Table 3.1: Integrity Core Value Rubric

The Lindsay Leader	The Passive Leader	The Underminer
• Thinks and acts according to high-level moral principles • Values are not changed by popular opinion • Is honest with self and others about issues • Acknowledges mistakes and tries to correct them • Consistently treats others with respect • Willing to take a stand based on principles and beliefs of the organization • Honors commitments • Works toward "win-win" • Honors and respects the core values of the organization • Does the right thing even when no one is looking • Passionate, brave, fair, and consistent	• Doesn't take a stand for a known wrong • Lacks courage • Settles for mediocrity out of fear of retribution or negative consequences • Knows right from wrong but fails to act	• Says one thing but does another • Uses their power inappropriately • Changes for personal gain or safety • Does not adhere to sound moral principles or ethics • Lies or tells partial truths • Prioritizes being politically correct over what's best for learners • Inconsistent and may say different things to different people • Shows favoritism • Dodges accountability • Selfish, self-serving • Bully

The rubrics provide a framework for the ideal Lindsay leader, whether that leader is a learner, learning facilitator, administrator, director, or other stakeholder. Individuals or groups can use them for personal reflection, to provide feedback, and to deepen commitment to these values. For example, in an early self-assessment, district leaders ranked themselves low on the core values of courage and risk taking. As a result, part of professional development for these leaders then focused on these two core values. Activities were designed and delivered to enhance team members' awareness of the importance of taking risks and being courageous, and team members shared and reinforced personal experiences. Six months later, the team self-rated with significantly higher scores in these core values.

Core values are the organizational norms in Lindsay Unified. Since their conception, the ten core values have not changed, and all members of the learning community have deepened their collective understanding of these values. In the district, if a staff member's behavior is inconsistent with the core values, it is likely that a colleague will address the misalignment by referencing the core value rubrics. For example, if a team member makes instructional decisions independent of team input, another team member would address it first by reminding that person of the exemplars for a Lindsay leader in teamwork— focusing on the good of the organization, considering viewpoints of all stakeholders, empowering others, and maximizing the capacity of team members.

In a more formal sense, the core values are a major component in the supervision and evaluation of key management positions. Such positions include site administrators, directors, and district leaders. As a supervisory tool, the core value rubrics provide the framework for behavior and guide each leader's actions. When improvement plans are established, the core values are front and center. The core values are not just something that staff members agree to in principle; they are the values by which those in Lindsay Unified live and work.

The Breakthrough Coach

The responsibilities that come with leading a school or district are complex and challenging, and success can be elusive. Many education leaders work fifty, sixty, or seventy hours per week and still are unable to show the achievement results they were hired to produce. The unfortunate reality is that many school and district leaders work very hard but often find themselves feeling completely overwhelmed and frustrated, as they are frequently engaged in tasks that have nothing to do with improving learning or developing staff. The common practice of giving one's whole life to a job ultimately has detrimental consequences for one's health, relationships, and general professional and personal wellness.

To better support its leaders, Lindsay Unified adopted the use of The Breakthrough Coach (Pancoast, 2011), a leadership enhancement approach for ensuring results, empowering educational leaders, and promoting general success for all staff members. The program is driven by the concept that in order to produce significant and sustainable results, everyone in the organization must be engaged in their work with the greatest levels of efficacy. Such effectiveness results when those in executive roles have the time, vision, energy, and focus to actually spend the majority of their time training and developing others' professional capabilities. The concept of executive as coach is essential because most successful people across professions have someone (a coach) who observes their performance (singing, playing a sport, producing movies, teaching, and so on) and provides feedback for validation and improvement. In the education world, the executives are principals, superintendents, directors, and managers—the people who lead and manage others in order to produce the desired results.

The sad reality is that, traditionally, people in these roles cannot or do not find the time or develop the skillset to improve the organization through the people they manage. Instead they become consumed by the workload. For example, many educational leaders (the executives) are consumed with technical work, such as responding to emails, typing memos, answering phones, and keeping track of paperwork. This leaves little time for leaders to visit learning communities, coach staff, or develop the people in administrative roles who are actually best suited to do the technical work. All Lindsay principals, directors, and district-level staff and their administrative assistants or secretaries are trained, coached, and supported in implementing breakthrough coach practices. A core principle of The Breakthrough Coach approach is that staff who act as managers and staff who act as technicians have distinct roles in the work of the organization. Technicians engage in all (or most) of the technical work, and managers (such as principals and directors) engage in the work of developing the professional and personal competence of those in their charge. As a result, school and district leaders now spend 60–80 percent of their time each week engaged in activities directly related to improving learner achievement and carrying out the mission and vision of the district.

When time, energy, and resources are committed to developing all parts of an organization, the organization is more efficient, and results are produced in all sectors of the organization. The commitment of Lindsay leaders and their administrative assistants to practicing the principles of The Breakthrough Coach has been essential to carrying out the education transformation that is still underway.

Collaborative Leadership Lindsay

The pathways toward leadership in public education are typically well defined and include traditional advanced degree programs, certificate programs, and professional development. However, there are many people in education who assume informal leadership roles without formal training. In addition, effective leadership looks different in the Performance Based System than it does in the traditional systems for which most leadership training programs are designed. It became important, therefore, to create a customized pathway to develop leadership skills and potential in all staff. This was the impetus for Collaborative Leadership Lindsay.

Collaborative Leadership Lindsay is a leadership development and support program designed to ensure the continuing vitality of Lindsay leadership, both throughout the city of Lindsay and within its school district. The program is designed to engage and develop existing and emerging leaders and motivate them to work together. The first cohort consisted of managers in teaching and nonteaching roles in the district, as well as management staff from the city of Lindsay. Subsequent cohorts have expanded to include office managers, maintenance and operations personnel, school psychologists, case managers, and local law enforcement. Each participant is nominated by his or her supervisor. The group meets each month for leadership training on topics that include communication and interpersonal dynamics, conducting effective meetings, conflict and human resource management, diversity, ethics, strategic planning, and finance. Additionally, each cohort plans and implements a community service project to demonstrate competence in collaboration, communication, and leadership. The first cohort organized a beautification project to renovate the Welcome to Lindsay signage, complete with landscaping, irrigation, and lighting. A later cohort committed to improving a city park. The program monitors its graduates to assess the impact of the training on their career trajectories and, for those from the district, on their efforts toward collaborative gains and leveraging opportunities to support the district's strategic design. Collaborative Leadership Lindsay continues to grow and develop leaders at all levels of the organization.

Summary

Transformational leadership in Lindsay evolved from many contributing aspects. With the strategic direction and strategic alignment as guiding forces from the strategic design, leadership components included organizational health, the core value rubrics, breakthrough coaching, and collaborative leadership. Just as Lindsay Unified created a vision for the district and its graduates, they created a vision for Lindsay leadership. This leadership is defined by strategic, purposeful behaviors and a collaborative capacity that builds effective teams. By distinguishing the exemplar Lindsay leader, the district prepared to continue the transformation with all personnel.

To transform leadership in the district, Lindsay Unified focused on the following areas.

- Developing strategic direction and alignment
- Developing and empowering leadership
- Focusing on professional outcomes and organizational health
- Developing core value rubrics for leadership

Elizabeth

Elizabeth transferred into Lindsay Unified as a fifth grader. The district's transformation to the Performance Based System was underway, and much of the language and systems were new to Elizabeth. She had never been in a school like the one she was in now. Leaders at many levels of the organization combined their efforts to ensure Elizabeth transitioned to her new environment successfully. Her learning facilitator communicated clear learning goals, created engaging learning experiences, and supported Elizabeth in becoming accountable for her own learning. Her principal communicated with Elizabeth and her family about how she was progressing and ways Elizabeth could benefit from continued after-school learning.

By seventh grade, Elizabeth felt like a new learner. Whereas she had once been shy and simply complied with teacher requests, in Lindsay's Performance Based System she became an advocate for her own education and moved through learning progressions with clarity and flexibility. When asked about her transition into Lindsay and her progress as a learner, she asserted, "When I take control of my learning, I take control of my life."

CHAPTER 4

Transforming Personnel

Lindsay Unified's Personnel Vision

- All Lindsay Unified staff, and especially learning facilitators, are hired, empowered, and retained because of their passion for educating children and young adults. Marginal staff members are given opportunities for development, and if they still do not meet district standards, they are helped to find employment elsewhere.

- Lindsay Unified is committed to the goal of having a professional staff that values, supports, and reflects the cultural diversity of the community and the learners that it serves.

- Lindsay Unified staff members are true professionals who reflect deeply upon their work—as individuals and as team members—and continually advance their knowledge and skills within their profession.

- Lindsay Unified staff members are caring, kind, consistent, respectful, and just in their interactions with learners. At the same time, staff members have high expectations and hold high standards for learners. This powerful combination of caring and holding high expectations leads to high learner performance.

continued ➔

- Learning facilitators and administrators know that learners learn in different ways, and sometimes, on different days. They are firm in what learners must ultimately demonstrate, but they are flexible regarding learning styles, learning rates, and manner of teaching.
- Learning facilitators, administrators, and the support staff take their role as models for youth seriously and behave accordingly.

Source: Lindsay Unified School District, 2007.

An intentional focus on realizing the district's vision for personnel has been key to the success of the Performance Based System in Lindsay Unified. Hiring the right people and investing in the development of each employee create a culture of empowerment that strengthens the overall level of commitment to the mission and vision of the organization. Leaders who are engaged in the work of recruiting, selecting, training, supporting, and retaining staff members embrace these responsibilities with the utmost care and seriousness. Because Lindsay Unified's vision calls for staff members to be caring, kind, consistent, respectful, and just, while also maintaining high expectations for all learners, personnel decisions are always driven by what is best for Lindsay learners. One essential piece of the personnel vision is that all staff—learning facilitators, administrators, and support staff—recognize their responsibility to be role models for youth and behave accordingly.

In this chapter, we discuss the changes to teacher roles required by the new system that support staff faced, as well as the overarching shift from teacher to learning facilitator.

Support Staff Aligned to the Lindsay Unified Vision

With the introduction of Lindsay Unified's Performance Based System, roles and expectations of all personnel changed dramatically, particularly for classified staff. *Classified staff* includes bus drivers, clerical staff, maintenance employees, food service employees, and those involved in learner supervision. In Lindsay Unified, classified staff are not often directly involved in instruction but are closely connected to the learning community's overall operations. These staff members have a daily impact and are often excellent role models for learners. In Lindsay Unified's new system, the traditional division between teaching staff and classified staff is left behind—all personnel are collectively committed to the mission of the district and focus their respective responsibilities on making the vision a reality. In fact, the board of trustees has prioritized empowering classified staff to fully embrace their important role in supporting Lindsay learners.

An important first step in empowering classified staff was to encourage a new mindset that would influence how these staff members viewed their roles and responsibilities. The leadership team worked with all classified staff to shift from a mindset of "I'm coming here to do my job" to a mindset of "All of the work I do is linked closely to something that will ultimately benefit Lindsay learners." The leadership team desires to empower every classified staff member to realize that his or her support of learners helps achieve Lindsay's mission and vision. Bus drivers have daily interactions with regular groups of learners and ensure timely attendance and accountability. Food service staff members ensure learners have their basic nutritional needs met before they attempt a day of mastery learning. After-school program leaders ensure learners continue to have engaging and relevant learning experiences even after the scheduled school day. Office managers ensure learning facilitators and parents have the information they need to successfully create and communicate learning experiences and opportunities. Every classified staff member at every level contributes to the success of Lindsay learners.

To support this new mindset, the superintendent holds biannual meetings with influential classified staff members to celebrate successes, listen to concerns, and answer questions. These meetings provide an excellent forum for classified staff members to experience validation, receive support, and develop a deeper level of commitment to the services they provide to Lindsay learners. Additionally, the district leadership team has committed significant resources and time to providing classified staff with relevant and ongoing professional development.

Such professional development includes training on the strategic design and its relation to their job descriptions, development of interpersonal skills in the workplace, how to use new technologies and cloud-based platforms, and collaborative work methods to increase achievement and productivity.

Because all staff have come to embrace the belief that learning happens in every corner of the learning community, all classified staff feel a responsibility for creating an environment that ensures that learners leave school wanting to return the next day. Communication between certified and classified staff is strong, and camaraderie, trust, and teamwork are central to the collective work. In the words of one staff member who serves lunches in the cafeteria, "I don't feel any less valued or respected because I work for food service. We are all treated the same, and we are all on the same team."

The Shift From Teacher to Learning Facilitator

Prior to Lindsay Unified's transition to the Performance Based System, the teacher was in control of the classroom and everything that was taught within it—a common practice in schools across the country. With the transformation, Lindsay leaders were asking teaching staff to disengage from past practice. The image of a teacher at the front of the room, imparting knowledge to students, is deeply ingrained in the minds of many educators because of what they experienced as learners themselves. Indeed, many Lindsay learning facilitators report that the most challenging aspect of the shift in their role was giving up sole ownership of the teaching and learning process.

The role of the traditional teacher has changed dramatically with the implementation of Lindsay Unified's Performance Based System. The teacher is now a facilitator of learning who tailors instruction to the abilities, interests, and preferences of learners and creates an environment in which learners are partners in the learning process. The learning facilitator's central role is to ensure that learning takes place using a combination of strategic and direct instruction, collaborative learning experiences, and customized curricula and assessment. No longer does the teacher station him- or herself at the front of the room. Instead, the learning facilitator moves through the room with the ebb and flow of the learning experiences necessitated by the learners. The learning facilitator can give feedback and respond to learners' needs in real time, and he or she can ensure differentiated learning that offers novelty, complexity, and depth. For example, a learning facilitator working on mathematics fluency with learners can group learners by their progress and learning needs. Rather than directing from the front of the classroom, the learning facilitator can work alongside learners to develop their proficiency and conduct assessments on demand. These flexible practices are in stark contrast to a traditional teacher who operates with predetermined lessons and assessment points that are unresponsive to the dynamics of learner needs.

Shifting teaching staff to the role of the learning facilitator occurred slowly, with both site leaders and learning facilitators on a steep learning curve. In order to realize the personnel vision for the district, site leaders and learning facilitators together had to build a strong foundation of trust, collaboration, and problem solving as they adopted the new vocabulary and took steps to translate language into action. Teachers who had long subscribed to traditional notions of pedagogy underwent identity shifts and adopted new perspectives about their practices. Through professional development, site and district leadership fostered this shift and encouraged open discussions and reflections about learning facilitators' new roles. Early adopters of Lindsay Unified's Performance Based System were not necessarily the most experienced teachers, but those who were willing to take risks. The district leadership team focused first on working with these more flexible learning facilitators, who, in turn, invited their colleagues into their classrooms to observe, learn, and provide feedback. As the systemic transformation progressed and learners became more empowered in their learning, the role of the teacher shifted naturally to that of a learning facilitator.

Next, we discuss the need for ongoing learning for personnel and the impact of the personnel vision on its learners.

Ongoing Learning for Lindsay Unified Personnel

All staff participate in intensive professional development to learn the foundations of performance-based education. Initial sessions focus on how to develop and communicate transparent learning outcomes, the calibration of mastery in content and level, pedagogy that serves learners in poverty, and the practices necessary to develop lifelong learners who are empowered in their learning. Integral to ongoing professional development is the mindset, derived from the strategic design and personnel vision, that all learning facilitators are leaders and deserve recognition as such. Empowered by this imperative, learning facilitators face the challenges of the Performance Based System with the same mindset they envision for their graduates—a mindset of perseverance and continuous improvement.

Supporting learning facilitators in continuing to refine their practice remains critical. Each summer, the district leadership team facilitates a learning symposium in which education experts offer active workshops related to implementation of the Performance Based System and personalized learning. Support and coaching are provided by the leadership team and external coaches. The district also employs instructional design and delivery specialists and blended learning assistants to coach and support various district initiatives.

The Impact of the Personnel Vision on Learners

Shifts in the roles of Lindsay Unified personnel have resulted in high levels of learner empowerment. The same empowerment that staff gain in the Performance Based System extends to the learners. Prior to Lindsay Unified's Performance Based System, the dominant modes of instruction in the district were lectures and repetitive skill sessions. Learning experiences revolved around short-term learning and surface-level assessments. Such techniques overly emphasized rote memorization. Absence rates were high, and within classes it was not unusual to observe compliant but disengaged learners. As personnel participated in systemic professional development, instruction became more learner centered, and the learning facilitators' high expectations fueled learners' intrinsic motivation. Changes in instruction and assessment shifted learner engagement from passivity to empowerment and advocacy.

Summary

In forging personnel practices guided by the strategic design, Lindsay Unified undertook an integral part of developing a new culture of learning. What once constituted successful staff no longer fostered the kind of environment Lindsay stakeholders envisioned. Instead, district leadership actively worked to transition staff at all levels into their new roles through a focused conceptualization of professional purpose as well as supportive and aligned professional development. Every staff member can discern the role he or she plays in learner achievement and how the shift to the Performance Based System transforms those roles. Just as instruction and learning evolve for learners, professional purpose and practices evolve for all staff members, challenging preconceived notions, testing their determination and perseverance, and instilling in them the same lifelong learning skillset that they seek to develop in learners.

In the process of transforming the roles of school personnel, Lindsay Unified took the following steps.

- Developing core values for all personnel
- Aligning all personnel to core values
- Developing a new mindset for all staff
- Providing support and training

Michael

To Michael, it felt like he had always had trouble in school. He struggled to comply with expectations and had little confidence in his own ability to succeed. He tried to fly under the radar, avoiding interactions with his teachers as they were negative more often than not. As Lindsay transitioned to the Performance Based System, Michael began to notice that not only his learning facilitators but also other staff were talking to him about his performance at school. What were once trips to the office due to misbehavior became discussions with his learning facilitator about what he needed to be successful and how he could have a more active role in his daily learning. When calls came home to his family, they were laced with reports of positive growth and behaviors. Even at lunch, the food services staff member asked how his classes were going as she filled his plate. It seemed everywhere Michael turned, school staff were demonstrating concern and consideration for his well-being.

Within the first two years of Lindsay's Performance Based System, Michael changed his behaviors in class, moved ahead of pace in his strongest subjects, and even voluntarily stayed after school to work with peers. Whereas he felt alienated and rejected by school staff in a traditional setting, in the Performance Based System he was motivated and supported. By graduation, he had a network of staff members that celebrated his success and encouraged him in his next steps and career goals.

CHAPTER 5

Transforming Curricula and Assessment

continued →

- The learner outcomes for Lindsay Unified focus on the whole child and learner; they ensure that each child and learner is prepared academically, socially, and emotionally. Lindsay Unified is concerned with what its learners know, what they are able to do, and what kinds of people they are becoming.

- Although Lindsay Unified does have some basic knowledge and skills that all graduates are expected to master, in most cases learner outcomes can be mastered accommodating the learning style and the interests of individual learners.

- Lindsay Unified learning facilitators and leaders are all future-focused trend trackers. Their study of the future allows them to update curriculum content when new and relevant content emerges. The same basic skills are then learned utilizing material that has meaning for everyone.

- Having second and third languages is valued and expected of all Lindsay graduates.

Source: Lindsay Unified School District, 2007.

Among the most necessary shifts in Lindsay Unified's transformation was the redesign of curricula and assessment. In looking at past practices, it was evident that the curriculum and assessment objectives lacked the viability, focus, relevance, and depth to ensure mastery of learning. In addition, the lack of transparency in the required learning at all levels left uncertainty in educators, learners, and families. The curriculum and assessment practices needed an overhaul that did not merely patch over the ineffectiveness but rather rebuilt it through the lens of competency-based learning.

As the foundation for the shift to mastery learning, every aspect of curricula and assessment underwent transformation. District leadership and learning facilitators faced the challenge of determining essential learning outcomes, establishing new methods to assess learning, and envisioning a curriculum that offers learners a personalized experience. Transformation to a personalized system of curricula and assessment is not possible without a set of transparent, clear, and viable learning outcomes.

In this chapter, we discuss the importance of having a guaranteed and viable curriculum in place before making any significant changes in instruction and the need for mastery-based assessment practices to improve student outcomes.

A Guaranteed and Viable Curriculum

Before making any significant instructional shifts, Lindsay Unified wanted to ensure that a rigorous curriculum was clearly defined. Leaders agreed that rather than trying to create a curriculum that addressed every single California State Standard, the district would collectively decide what was absolutely essential for learners to learn.

Narrowing the curriculum to essential knowledge and skills was extremely difficult, but it made the curriculum viable, meaning that it focuses only on the essential learning outcomes and encompasses a manageable amount of content. By working with a more focused curriculum, Lindsay Unified could also ensure that learners understood exactly what they were expected to know and be able to do. Including only the most essential learning made planning a learner-centered curriculum that emphasizes reasoning, problem solving, and communication a more feasible task. Because the curriculum is viable, the curriculum is also guaranteed, meaning that, without exception, every single learner will learn it. By streamlining the curriculum to a manageable amount of content and requiring mastery, the district has eliminated the variability that is often present in traditional systems.

Here, we discuss the importance of defining learning targets and creating lifelong learning standards.

Defining Learning Targets

The curriculum Lindsay Unified created is composed of *measurement topics*, or subject-specific units of study. Measurement topics are composed of a set of closely related learning targets. Each learning target is, in turn, divided into performance levels that reflect the 1–4 scoring scale used within the district. Within this scoring scale, level 3 content is the target content; when a learner achieves a score of 3, it signifies that he or she has achieved proficiency in that learning target. Level 2 contains the basic or foundational knowledge, and level 4 involves more advanced applications. Learning targets are either direct interpretations of state standards or a careful synthesis of standards to support the measurement topic construction. For example, a measurement topic in world history at the high school level titled "The Development of Modern Political Thought" includes learning targets on the major European political philosophers, foundational documents such as the Magna Carta and the Bill of Rights, and the political ideology of the French Revolution. These learning targets, housed in the measurement topic, form a unit that allows the learning facilitator to create learning experiences that address multiple state standards and support diverse avenues of learning, evidence, and assessment.

To design the measurement topics, leaders and learning facilitators worked together in core committees, guided by resources such as *Designing and Teaching Learning Goals & Objectives* (Marzano, 2009) and *A Different Kind of Classroom: Teaching with Dimensions of Learning* (Marzano, 1992). These teams worked for an entire year to unpack the California State Standards, identifying all learning as either simple or complex knowledge. After unpacking the standards, the teams created progressions of learning targets that populated the newly constructed measurement topics in language arts, mathematics, social studies, and science.

The curriculum for these core areas was piloted during the 2008–2009 school year and underwent revision over subsequent years as standards and state outcomes evolved. Once the essential curriculum in the four key subjects was identified, the committees turned their attention to developing measurement topics for electives (that is, music, art, physical education, health, foreign language, agriculture, technology, and industrial arts).

For each learning target, the team created a rubric that clearly identifies the components of mastery. Whereas the scoring scale helps differentiate the levels of learning in a measurement topic and learning target, the more specific rubrics help clarify learning and outcomes for each element of content. These rubrics and their descriptors are eminently useful in two specific ways.

1. First, the rubrics inform learners exactly what they are expected to learn and demonstrate for each target. Rubrics empower the learner to gauge his or her own progress and enable peer feedback and scoring.

2. Second, the rubrics ensure consistency across the district in assessing learner performance and levels.

After constructing rubrics, learning facilitators and district staff began the task of designing formative assessments and district benchmarks. Staff also identified resources, materials, instructional strategies, and engagement techniques. These materials and strategies, selected according to learning targets, are flexible so as to accommodate different interests and learning styles. Using formal and informal assessment measures, as well as district assessments, learners and learning facilitators track progress toward mastery of each measurement topic. For each measurement topic, learning facilitators use a cycle of instruction, assessment, and feedback until learners can adequately demonstrate at least level 3 knowledge and skill. Lindsay Unified continues to ensure that all stakeholders across the district clearly understand what is expected for mastery.

Creating Lifelong Learning Standards

Leaders and stakeholders in Lindsay felt strongly that, in addition to addressing academic learning, the district's curriculum should address the skills that learners need in order to be successful in the 21st century. As part of the new strategic vision, Lindsay Unified crafted a set of lifelong learning standards that identify what learners need to know, understand, and do in order to thrive. These standards describe the types of human beings that Lindsay Unified's Performance Based System strives to produce: people who are well balanced, self-directed, compassionate, civic minded, and culturally aware, and who are global citizens, quality producers, and good resource managers. To ensure that these critical dispositions were an integral part of the curriculum,

Lindsay Unified designed measurement topics that identify personal attributes that it considered essential to each of these orientations. Rubrics were established for each of the seven spheres of living (see pages 33–34). For example, for the personal sphere learning target that relates to managing behavior and emotions, the rubric begins with learners at the kindergarten level demonstrating they can make observations about emotions and their effects on others. By upper elementary, learners progress into analyzing the factors that contribute to stress and various emotions so that by high school they can identify and utilize strategies to regulate emotion during unexpected situations and events. Each measurement topic in the lifelong learning spheres is unpacked in similar detail to ensure learners can achieve mastery.

In addition to being transparently defined, Lindsay Unified's lifelong learning standards are reported separately from academic scores. This prevents one of the problems of traditional grading systems, which is that grades often do not reflect a learner's actual level of knowledge and skill because they are confounded by participation grades, work completion grades, and the like. Rather than blend the scoring for lifelong learning into academic achievement, the district provides a separate method for scoring these targets in the learning management system to ensure parents and families distinctly recognize each learner's academic status and growth and his or her development as a lifelong learner. Moreover, as part of the district's graduation requirements, learners must demonstrate proficiency in every measurement topic associated with the lifelong learning standards.

Lifelong learning measurement topics, like their academic counterparts, compose core competencies that ensure Lindsay graduates attain college and career readiness. While defining the competencies and articulating them for all stakeholders were critical in the shift to the Performance Based System and at the heart of the curriculum and assessment work, it was the move to ensure mastery that challenged the boundaries of traditional systems and academic achievement.

Mastery-Based Assessment Practices

Lindsay Unified's Assessment Vision

- Learner assessment is directly aligned with district learning outcomes. Lindsay Unified identifies what learners need to know, to be able to do, and to be like. It teaches identified learner outcomes and assesses learner progress based on those desired outcomes. That is, there is direct alignment among learner outcomes, instruction, and learner assessment.

- Lindsay learners are allowed and encouraged to demonstrate their learning in various ways. Written tests are not the dominant manner for assessing learning. Learner performances are very popular and are emphasized.

- Meeting individual learning needs allows Lindsay Unified to have high expectations for learner achievement. Curriculum, instruction, and assessment practices are rigorous, ensuring that Lindsay learners will be successful in colleges and universities or in whatever life they pursue after leaving Lindsay.

- Although the district's learning facilitators do not "teach for the test," Lindsay learners perform well when compared to students in other California schools and nationally.

Source: Lindsay Unified School District, 2007.

In Lindsay's Performance Based System, assessment is tightly integrated with learning. In the cycle of instruction, assessment is used to show evidence of learning and to shape future instruction. In this way, the model directly connects learner outcomes, instruction, and assessment. The transparency of multiple data sources ensures that learners and parents accurately understand learner progress. This knowledge helps learners self-evaluate, provides clear direction for advancement, or reveals a need for additional support. Learner assessment provides important feedback, fosters intrinsic motivation, and informs instructional decisions. In addition, assessments contribute to overall program evaluation.

Diagnostic and Formative Assessments

Assessments provide learners, learning facilitators, and other stakeholders with information that can guide learning-oriented action. Generally speaking, Lindsay Unified relies on two types of assessments: (1) diagnostic assessments and (2) formative assessments.

To determine placement, learners are given diagnostic assessments. This type of assessment is a pretest that identifies a learner's current level of proficiency in a particular content area. These diagnostic assessments are used during three specific times: (1) when learners first join the district, (2) during districtwide assessment windows during the school year, and (3) as learners progress into new content areas and levels. Based on the results of diagnostic assessments, Lindsay learners are assigned to appropriate levels of difficulty in each subject area, commonly referred to as *content levels*. For example, one learner's personalized learning plan may include instruction in English at content level 4, mathematics at content level 7, science at content level 5, and social studies at content level 6. Once a learner is placed at a content level, learning facilitators use daily and weekly formative assessments to measure the learner's progress toward higher levels of proficiency in particular topics, creating an evolving personalized learning plan. When formative assessment data indicate that a learner may be ready to progress to the next content level, a districtwide benchmark assessment (see page 70) is administered to ensure mastery.

Formative assessments are those that provide information to the learner and the learning facilitator about a learner's progress toward a particular learning target. Formative assessment is both a process and the products of that process. As a process, formative assessment is any activity that provides evidence regarding a learner's progress toward a particular learning goal. Formative assessments demonstrate that the cycle of instruction and feedback has resulted in measurable evidence toward mastery. The process of formative assessment (closely tied to the instructional cycle, page 83) includes the following.

- **Identifying the current learning target:** Ensuring learners know what they are learning and why

- **Engaging in activities that generate evidence regarding learner progress:** Learning experiences co-constructed by the learning facilitator and learner to gain and apply both simple and complex knowledge

- **Analyzing the evidence:** A process that involves both the learning facilitator and the learner considering rubrics and evidence to discern what progress has been made thus far

- **Providing corrective feedback to the learner:** A dialogue between the learning facilitator and the learner to continue the learning cycle and ensure mastery

- **Reflecting on instructional practice:** The learning facilitator considering which instructional techniques and practices best serve learners in their progress toward mastery and how to ensure similar success in subsequent learning experiences

The process and products of formative assessment ensure that learning facilitators can identify learners who have demonstrated proficiency, who need additional support, or who possibly need alternative methods to demonstrate learning.

Because learners learn in different ways and on different schedules, Lindsay Unified's philosophy about assessment is that there are various methods of demonstrating learning. Although written tests are used, learners have opportunities to demonstrate learning in other ways. Ideally, assessments are performance based and take a range of modalities and learning styles into consideration. For example, assessments may include multiple methods of personal communication, such as engaging in conferencing or writing responses to literature. Learners may demonstrate understanding by performing plays, poems, or podcasts; engaging in debates, role plays, or simulations; or presenting information in oral, visual, or multimedia forms. Learners may create projects, conduct observations, or design a portfolio. In sum, assessment may be anything the learner said, did, or created to show evidence of learning.

A distinguishing characteristic of Lindsay Unified's Performance Based System is the elimination of formal summative assessments. In a traditional system, summative assessments (such as final exams) are used in isolation to assign final grades at the ends of units, semesters, or academic years. In Lindsay Unified, shifting from summative to formative assessments reflects the core belief in a growth mindset—all students are capable of achieving mastery. In the district's Performance Based System, learning is ongoing—once proficiency is demonstrated on a particular measurement topic, learners advance to the next measurement topic. Because there is no designated end of learning within the academic year, there are no specific summative assessments for all learners; however, there are benchmark assessments, which are also used in a formative manner.

Benchmark Assessments

To tightly align the rigor of assessments and instruction, Lindsay Unified initially designed *benchmark assessments*—assessments given at key points in a learner's academic progress to inform and tailor instruction to the learner's needs. These assessments determine proficiency at various levels and establish consistency in regard to academic rigor. The district assessment team streamlined these assessments to ensure a focus on the quality, rather than the quantity, of evidence of learning. A standard operating procedure was developed that requires that learners produce evidence of learning before taking a benchmark assessment. The benchmark assessment, by the nature of its design, verifies mastery or indicates a need for continued instruction. As such, learning facilitators approach it with prior formative assessment experiences to ensure learners are ready for the assessment and can demonstrate learning.

In some situations, learners can use the benchmark assessment as a challenge test, allowing them to progress to the next learning target. Early on in the transformation, these benchmark assessments became one of the first ways learners could move ahead of their traditional age-based grade levels. This method of allowing learners to use benchmark assessments safeguarded against learners spending time on measurement topics and learning targets that they had already mastered.

Grading and Scoring

As previously noted, Lindsay Unified's curriculum involves learning targets articulated at four levels of performance. Accordingly, the traditional grading system has been replaced with a more meaningful and accurate four-point scoring scale. Lindsay Unified's Performance Based System also separates academic grades from nonacademic grades through the use of two distinct scoring scales (figures 5.1 and 5.2). On the academic scoring scale, a score of 1 or 2 indicates that learning is in progress but learners have not yet mastered the content. A score of 3 indicates proficiency, and a score of 4 reflects deeper application of knowledge. Half-point scores of 1.5, 2.5, and 3.5 indicate performance that exceeds one level but does not quite reach the next level. The scale, transparent to all stakeholders, creates a common language of proficiency. It is the crux of the shift to competency-based learning.

Score	What the Learner Knows
4	The learner knows all of the simple knowledge and skills and all of the complex knowledge and skills, and goes beyond what was taught in class to apply the knowledge.
3.5	The learner knows all of the simple knowledge and skills and all of the complex knowledge and skills, and can make in-depth inferences and applications with partial success.
3	The learner knows all of the simple knowledge and skills and all of the complex knowledge and skills.
2.5	The learner knows all of the simple knowledge and skills and some of the complex knowledge and skills.
2	The learner knows all of the simple knowledge and skills.
1.5	The learner knows some of the simple knowledge and skills and some of the complex knowledge and skills.
1	With help, the learner knows some of the simple and complex knowledge and skills.

Figure 5.1: Lindsay Unified scoring scale for academic learning.

A second scoring scale reflects Lindsay Unified's lifelong learning standards (see figure 5.2 on page 72). These standards are the socioemotional learning curriculum in the district and are considered just as important as academic learning. Teachers have established rubrics for each of the seven spheres of living, and learners must demonstrate proficiency in every measurement topic associated with each lifelong learning standard as part of their graduation requirements. At its essence, this scale institutes a process for learners to gain key socioemotional competencies by moving through the spheres in the same fluid and flexible progression as academic learning. Like academic achievement, becoming a lifelong learner does not occur at the same rate for each learner, and the scale is designed to reflect the individualized path each learner will take to proficiency.

Score	What the Learner Does
4	The learner demonstrates learning above and beyond proficiency.
3	The learner demonstrates proficiency.
2	The learner is progressing toward proficiency.
1	The learner is beginning the process toward proficiency.

Figure 5.2: Lindsay Unified scoring scale for lifelong learning standards.

Learning facilitators score learner performance on the scales both to give feedback during the learning process and to determine mastery. To determine a score, a learning facilitator compares evidence from an assessment to the rubric for the relevant learning goal. If the learner's performance seems to demonstrate mastery, the learning facilitator uses the criteria at level 3 on the scale to verify that score. If the learner is still working toward proficiency, the learning facilitator determines whether the learner independently knows the simple content described by level 2 or needs help to show any knowledge or skill (level 1). If the learner has mastered the level 3 knowledge and skill and can apply it in ways that were not directly taught, the learning facilitator assigns a score of 4.

These four-point scales are crucial to the Performance Based System because, by definition, the system requires a grading structure that clearly defines mastery. Scales and rubrics for each learning target identify unambiguous goals and explicit intermediate steps toward those goals. The four-point scale makes progress and mastery transparent to learners and their parents. In addition, level 4 of the scale allows learners to demonstrate knowledge or skill that goes beyond proficiency, which motivates and encourages students to exceed expectations academically and in life.

Translating Lindsay Unified's Performance-Based Grading System

While Lindsay Unified is fully committed to personalized learning, the reality is that the majority of educational institutions outside the district do not fully understand performance-based grading. The educational system outside of Lindsay still uses traditional letter grades, grade point averages, class rankings, and course requirements for entrance into colleges and universities. Early on, Lindsay Unified recognized the need to translate learner performance outcomes and proficiency levels so that Lindsay learners could easily transfer to traditional schools, meet college entrance requirements, and qualify for various scholarships.

Administrators developed a simple conversion factor to translate the district's performance levels into a grade point average accepted by outside institutions. This conversion ensures learners have applicable evidence of college readiness. A score of 4, considered more extensive and rigorous learning and application, translates to an A+. A score of 3.5 equates to an A-. The level 3 learning, the required proficiency in Lindsay's Performance Based System, translates to a B. Learners graduating from Lindsay's Performance Based System leave with a grade point average that represents not only their proficiency, but also whether they have chosen to exceed that proficiency.

Once they have learned about Lindsay Unified's grading system, most colleges and universities have indicated that they greatly prefer the competency-based accountability system to traditional grading. They know that grades across different high schools, and even across different teachers, within a traditional educational system are not comparable because proficiency is often not well defined and traditional grading systems are highly subjective. On many occasions, colleges have given Lindsay's graduating seniors preference in acceptance because of the consistency and integrity that are foundational to the Performance Based System.

Summary

In the effort to build a new system of education, Lindsay worked extensively to transform traditional notions of curricula and assessment. Through collaborative efforts and a strategic approach to state standards and expectations, district leadership and learning facilitators brought forth a new framework of their own design. This framework channeled essential learning into viable measurement topics that both learning facilitators and learners could use within a flexible instructional cycle. The structure of the measurement topics derived from a common scoring scale and rubrics that delineated precise descriptions of proficiency. The assessment of these topics and learning targets followed suit. The assessment process, predominantly diagnostic and formative, supports instruction and assures learners receive the feedback and continuous learning experiences necessary for proficiency. Lifelong learning, a critical component of the guaranteed and viable curriculum, also came to fruition with measurement topics and a scoring scale, offering learners a path to socioemotional proficiency in tandem with their academic achievement. The initiative to transform curricula and assessment became the natural springboard for continued progress, which included a transformation of the teaching and learning cycle.

In order to transform the curriculum for its Performance Based System, Lindsay Unified took the following steps.

- Defining essential learning
- Developing measurement topics
- Developing rubrics and progressions
- Activating learners at appropriate content levels
- Developing socioemotional learning outcomes

The district also transformed its assessment practices in the following ways.

- Integrating assessments with the instructional model
- Determining assessment types
- Determining instructional uses for assessments
- Correlating assessments to scoring scales

Mayra

Prior to Lindsay Unified's Performance Based System, Mayra knew she wanted to someday go to college and become a doctor. She hoped that the grades she was getting would help her do that. Her family, first-generation immigrants, supported her goals and encouraged her to succeed in school, but Mayra wasn't sure she knew what it would take to get to college.

With the new grading model, Mayra learned quickly what it meant to master content and achieve a higher level of learning. By eighth grade, she was considered "a fast runner" by her learning facilitator. She worked consistently to master measurement topics and sought out feedback from her learning facilitator on how she could deepen her learning. After being reclassified from the status of an English learner, she assessed out of all eighth-grade ELA measurement topics and completed many level 4 learning projects. Her learning facilitator, wanting to ensure Mayra had continued learning opportunities, worked with learning facilitators at the high school to ensure Mayra had access to advanced learning experiences. With the support of both learning communities, Mayra attended English language arts classes at the high school twice a week. In addition, her high school learning facilitator exposed her to college entry requirements that she could begin addressing in eighth grade.

CHAPTER 6

Transforming Teaching and Learning

continued →

> • Learning opportunities seldom follow a single traditional field of study. Most frequently, learners will be learning math, science, language arts, and social science while analyzing and solving real-life problems in today's world.
>
> • Because Lindsay Unified customizes learning to the individual learner, grade levels have been eliminated. The question is no longer "Is Betty ready for the fifth grade?" but, instead, "Which learning outcome is Betty ready for now?"

Source: Lindsay Unified School District, 2007.

With a new curricular framework in place, Lindsay Unified was prepared to tackle the delivery of instruction. The vision, as outlined by the strategic design, was for Lindsay learners to have instructional experiences that pushed learning beyond the walls of the classroom, contextualized it with projects and community engagement, and harnessed the power of technology and the Internet.

To engender such a reality, Lindsay Unified had to articulate what such a model would look like in learners' everyday experiences. The learning facilitators who pioneered the Performance Based System were key personnel in delineating this reality. Their learning environments served as testing grounds for new teaching practices, methods of grouping learners, differentiated instruction, and engagement. They also explored new ways to monitor academic progress and enable learner accountability and advocacy. Feedback from these learning facilitators also informed how the instructional model, in alignment with the strategic design, would come to life.

In this chapter, we discuss the leaders' intensive focus on instruction, the components of Lindsay's instructional model, the importance of engaging learners, how differentiation factors in, and the role of technology in the systemic shift.

Intensive Focus on Instruction

Once first drafts of the curriculum were created, leaders began an intensive focus on instruction. Research shows that the learning facilitator's professional decisions in the classroom are the factor that most impacts learner achievement (Marzano, 2003, 2007), so it is essential that learning facilitators become instructional experts. Top priorities for instruction were engaging learners, setting clear goals for learning, and using proven classroom strategies. With these priorities in mind, Lindsay Unified created an instructional model comprised of research-based instructional strategies and provided ongoing professional development to support leaders and learning facilitators.

Through the support of Bea McGarvey, Susana Dutro, and several other instructional experts, the leadership team engaged in comprehensive professional development to more clearly understand the characteristics of quality instruction. The team also worked with experts on the Common Core State Standards for English language arts and mathematics, as well as experts in English language development, to deepen their understanding. Through the process of learning about high-quality instruction, the team focused on building competence, using guiding texts including *Classroom Instruction That Works: Research-Based Strategies for Increasing Student Achievement* (Marzano, Pickering, & Pollock, 2001), *Dimensions of Learning: Teacher's Manual* (Marzano & Pickering, 1997), and *The Art and Science of Teaching: A Comprehensive Framework for Effective Instruction* (Marzano, 2007).

Overall, leaders and learning facilitators engaged in several hundred hours of professional development focused on quality instruction. The leadership team then synthesized key learning from the professional development to create instructional models for each content area, which were then disseminated to learning communities by each site principal. Through this extensive professional development, Lindsay Unified established a common language of instruction. The common language, built into the structures of learning, assured all learning facilitators could deliver quality instruction and support learners at all levels in Lindsay's Performance Based System.

Lindsay Unified's Instructional Model

Lindsay Unified's instructional model provides a common language that unifies the district's instructional vision and ensures the alignment of instructional decisions with this vision. The instructional model in Lindsay Unified has three main components: (1) systems of learning, (2) the cycle of instruction, and (3) research-based instructional strategies.

Systems of Learning

Marzano and Kendall's (2007) model of mental processing describes a hierarchy of three systems of thinking involved in completing tasks and using knowledge. First, the *self system*—which contains one's beliefs, goals, and desires—decides whether or not to engage in a task. Then, the *metacognitive system* sets goals and selects the best strategies for completing the task. Finally, the *cognitive system* processes information relevant to the task. Instruction in Lindsay Unified engages all three systems of learning.

The cognitive system includes four levels of cognitive processes: (1) retrieving, (2) comprehending, (3) analyzing, and (4) utilizing knowledge. To develop and support a healthy cognitive system, lessons are designed to ensure the alignment of cognitive complexity and the learning goal. By unpacking standards and aligning their rigor with these four levels, learning facilitators can create learning goals at various levels that ensure learners access both declarative and procedural knowledge. Academic knowledge is applied in complex tasks, such as comparing and contrasting, hypothesizing, generalizing, and predicting. These learning goals, supported by diagnostic and formative assessments, guide instruction and learning.

The metacognitive system regulates cognitive processes, with a focus on setting learning goals, monitoring thinking processes, and deepening understanding. Basically, learners need to think about their thinking. In Lindsay Unified, learning facilitators promote a healthy metacognitive system by helping learners master the skills of monitoring their thinking, evaluating the effectiveness of their actions, and choosing appropriate strategies to accomplish particular goals. Learners work through processes that help them understand how they learn best and why. Through reflection, goal setting, and dialogue with learning facilitators, learners can identify their best learning styles, anticipate academic struggles, and discover where and why mastery is occurring so they can apply it to other curricular areas. For example, a fifth-grade learner who discovers she is a visual and verbal learner can apply those styles of learning to other topics and set goals to both learn and produce evidence of learning through those modes. Within this system, learning facilitators help learners develop stamina and perseverance, engage in activities to push the limits of their learning, develop disciplined thinking and action, and learn to view situations from multiple perspectives.

The self system encompasses learner attitudes toward and perceptions of learning and particular learning tasks. It entails the preconceived notions learners have about learning and school, their own intelligences, and the value of learning itself. It is one of the most important and early indicators of where learners need support and their prior academic and socioemotional struggles and successes. Helping learners cultivate a healthy self system entails creating a classroom climate that is nurturing and safe, that fosters positive relationships between learning facilitators and learners as well as among peers, and that ensures an orderly and predictable classroom structure. Learning facilitators also must ensure that learners find classroom tasks to be interesting, valuable, and appropriately challenging. For example, as part of establishing the culture that supports the development of a healthy self system, learning facilitators begin the year by co-constructing a shared vision and code of cooperation with learners. Instead of establishing an environment that has rules and punitive consequences, learning facilitators guide learners to design their own norms for the learning environment. This voice and feedback then extends into the learning experiences. Because the environment is one of dual ownership between the learning facilitator and learners, the daily cycle of instruction becomes equally empowered. Learners can voice feedback on their learning, seek support freely, and learn at the level they need to in order to progress. Learning facilitators, in response to such interaction, build around the academic needs of the learners. To promote a healthy self system, learning facilitators ensure that learners clearly understand the learning objective and have the resources necessary to complete all tasks successfully.

One of the most important aspects of the self system is developing a growth mindset. According to Carol Dweck (2006), the growth mindset challenges the notions that ability is fixed and people have limitations in what they can learn. Instead, when learners and educators have a growth mindset, they understand that people can develop intelligence. Learners focus on improvement instead of worrying about how smart they are. They understand that they can work hard and improve their performance. In Lindsay Unified's Performance Based System, all stakeholders explicitly teach, model, and reinforce the growth mindset. Learning facilitators also engage the growth mindset to challenge their own fixed views on teaching and learning. By working with learners to shift their mindset, learning facilitators also expand their understanding of what works best for learners, how instruction can adapt to learner needs, and the need for perseverance and flexibility in learning. The growth mindset is a contributing factor in establishing high expectations for all learners, staff, and stakeholders and is a crucial part of how Lindsay's culture of learning shifted with the transformation to its Performance Based System.

The Cycle of Instruction

In Lindsay Unified, learning facilitators utilize a cycle of instruction. The cycle has six steps (see figure 6.1).

1. Teach to a learning goal.
2. Assess learner progress.
3. Analyze results.
4. Provide feedback.
5. Respond to feedback.
6. Reteach as needed.

This cyclical model is driven by learner data, precise goals, and instructional planning. The learner's empowerment and accountability are a key part of this cycle. Because learners interact with learning facilitators at each point, the burden of accountability shifts from being solely the adult's role to being a partnership between learner and educator. The goal setting, feedback, and tracking of learning are an ongoing dialogue that requires learners to know what they are learning, why they are learning it, and how much progress they've accomplished toward the goal.

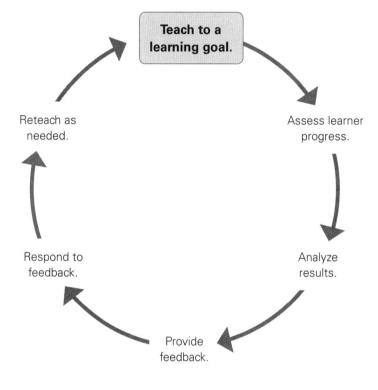

Figure 6.1: The cycle of instruction.

Every lesson is driven by a learning goal, which is clearly communicated, understood, and tracked by the learner and the learning facilitator. Learners own their learning goals. During goal setting, learners understand what is required to demonstrate proficiency and mastery. The first stage of the instructional cycle involves teaching and learning toward that goal. Learners are empowered to learn independently through technology, experiences, or exploration, especially in the case of simple knowledge (level 2 content). Learning facilitators also use a variety of grouping and instructional strategies to help learners acquire knowledge.

In the second stage, learners and learning facilitators use a variety of formative assessment strategies to assess progress. Assessments are not all traditional pencil-and-paper tests; many are demonstrations of knowledge or performance. Assessment results are transparent to the learner and to the learning facilitator. The next step of the cycle is to analyze the assessment data to glean information about the quality of instruction and to provide feedback to the learner. Once the learning facilitator has a clear understanding of a learner's progress, specific and personal feedback is delivered so that the learner can also understand his or her current progress and develop a plan for moving forward. The learning facilitator then adapts his or her instructional strategies, using learner performance data to guide differentiation and grouping and regrouping.

For example, if a learner is attempting mastery of a measurement topic on narrative writing, the first formative assessment is scored on a rubric that assesses content, English conventions, and cohesion. With the rubric, the learning facilitator meets with the learner to give feedback on specific areas of improvement and develop a plan for instruction. That plan can include the learner working with a peer on specific areas, such as the conventions of spelling and capitalization. The plan can also include small-group instruction with other learners who need support developing the content of their narrative writing. The plan would also mandate another formative assessment experience after the learner has benefitted from instruction and differentiated learning experiences. The cycle of instruction, each time it takes a revolution, serves to focus on what learners need in a personalized and data-driven manner.

This cycle of instruction is driven by an intentional focus on results. Through the cycle of instruction, the learner remains invested in his or her learning, tracking progress toward the learning goal and celebrating success. The learner repeats the cycle until he or she demonstrates mastery, and then begins again with a new learning target.

Research-Based Instructional Strategies

The third component of the instructional model is research-based instructional strategies. Rather than assume all learning facilitators knew what would work best, the district actively sought out practices with proven track records of success with learner populations like those in Lindsay. For learning facilitators to develop the cognitive, metacognitive, and self systems in learners through the instructional cycle, they needed a toolbox of strategies that were both effective and amenable to the Performance Based System.

Early on, the district embraced research-based strategies such as those described in *Classroom Instruction That Works* (Marzano, Pickering, & Pollock, 2001), which focused on how learners can take control of their education, engage in metacognitive processes, and process new learning. Critical strategies included note taking and summarizing because of their applicability to multiple content areas and levels and the support they provided to the development of learners' cognitive systems. Goal setting and reflection were also important strategies because they foster the development of learners' metacognitive and self systems (Marzano, 2003). Over time, further study by the district indicated that some of the strategies had a positive effect on learner achievement in some situations, but not in others. This further study suggested that, rather than assuming that all proven instructional strategies would be effective for all learners, learning facilitators should rely on their knowledge of the learner, the subject matter, and the context to identify the most appropriate strategies for each learner.

Currently, the district is integrating the work of John Hattie and the concept of visible learning. Hattie explained:

> Visible teaching and learning occurs when there is deliberate practice aimed at attaining mastery of the goal, when there is feedback given and sought, and when there are active, passionate, and engaging people (teacher, students, peers) participating in the act of learning. (2012, p. 18)

Hattie systematically studied the effect sizes of different instructional strategies on learner achievement. Effect size is one method that education researchers use to answer the question, "What has the greatest influence on learning?" In Lindsay Unified, learning communities work in site-based achievement teams to plan, monitor, and adjust instruction to ensure learner achievement, and choose instructional strategies according to effect size. Among the most prominent strategies from

Hattie's research that are utilized in Lindsay learning environments and the cycle of instruction are feedback, metacognitive strategies, direct instruction, peer tutoring, cooperative learning, and integrated and computer-assisted instruction. Based on Hattie's (2012) reported effect sizes, learning facilitators harness the power of research in their learning environments for learners' academic achievement. These evidence-based strategies are powerful tools for instructional planning and delivery.

In addition to individual instructional strategies, learning facilitators also plan instruction using ten essential questions from *The Art and Science of Teaching* (Marzano, 2007).

1. What will I do to establish and communicate learning goals, track progress, and celebrate success?

2. What will I do to help learners effectively interact with new knowledge?

3. What will I do to help learners practice and deepen their understanding of new knowledge?

4. What will I do to help learners generate and test hypotheses about new knowledge?

5. What will I do to engage learners?

6. What will I do to establish or maintain learning environment rules and procedures?

7. What will I do to recognize and acknowledge adherence and lack of adherence to learning environment rules and procedures?

8. What will I do to establish and maintain effective relationships with learners?

9. What will I do to communicate high expectations for all learners?

10. What will I do to develop effective lessons organized into a cohesive unit?

These questions reflect the core ideas of Lindsay Unified's Performance Based System. For example, the first question—What will I do to establish and communicate learning goals, track progress, and celebrate success?—emphasizes the need to ensure that learners know what they are expected to know and do in reference to a particular learning target, that they can determine where they are in relation to that goal, and that their ability to demonstrate mastery is recognized. These questions are at the root of all systems in the learning environment, of communication and feedback at all levels, and of the critical rapport that learning facilitators develop with learners.

The Engaging of Learners

Lindsay Unified's Learning Vision

- Every day, Lindsay learners come to school and are met at their developmental learning levels; they are challenged, they are successful, and they leave school each day wanting to return the next day.

- All Lindsay learners are highly motivated to learn because the learning experiences for each one are matched to his or her developmental learning level, learning styles and strengths, and interests.

- Lindsay learners believe that today's world requires lifelong learning, and learning facilitators design learning activities to ensure that graduates leave the school system as self-directed, future-focused, lifelong learners. As Lindsay learners advance through programs, they increasingly become accountable for their own learning.

- Our world is becoming increasingly global and diverse, and Lindsay learners continuously learn to embrace diversity—diversity of cultures, religions, ethnicities, and ways of viewing the world.

- All Lindsay learners leave the school system with the opportunity to choose the future that they desire; graduates are ready for college, for employment, or for creatively designing their own future.

- Lindsay Unified has become recognized as the place to visit to watch learners and adults study, analyze, and debate cultural, religious, economic, and global issues.

Source: Lindsay Unified School District, 2007.

The traditional educational system often produces compliant and complacent learners who are not invested in their learning. As Lindsay Unified transitioned to personalized learning, many learners initially lacked the skills and experience to be active learners. Learning facilitators' early focus on using engagement strategies taught these learners to be attentive, focused, and active in the learning environment. This included allowing students' input in determining the norms of the learning environment, explicit instruction on goal setting and reflection, and encouraging students to seek out topics of interest that could be integrated into learning. Learners, who had once been told what and how to learn, were encouraged to express how they learn best and what interested them most.

Even the structure of the learning environment has changed in the new wave of personalization. Rows of desks that isolate learners and prevent discussion and cooperative learning have been replaced by learning environments focused on collaborative setups; the placement of technology and the facilitation of small-group instruction are essential. The updated learning environments prioritize collaboration between learners, methods of tracking learning, and venues for varied modes of instruction.

By design, Lindsay Unified's Performance Based System pushes to deepen learner engagement. All learners experience strong levels of motivation and empowerment because they are met at their developmental levels, they are challenged, and they ultimately experience success. To support the shift to a learner-focused model, learning facilitators also changed the ways in which they designed classroom procedures and interactions. In a traditional classroom, a teacher normally creates his or her own vision regarding how learners will behave and engage in activities, perhaps drafting a list of rules and routines prior to the start of school and sharing it with learners on the first day of class. In Lindsay Unified's Performance Based System, learning facilitators and learners in each learning environment work together to construct a shared contract so that learners and learning facilitators have an equal investment in the way learning interactions are structured. For example, the stakeholders of each learning environment create a code of collaboration that spells out norms and agreements for how learners and learning facilitators will work together. Learners, because they have ownership of the code of collaboration, hold one another responsible and accountable and self-reflect on their adherence to the agreement. This promotes learner agency, personal responsibility, and full empowerment in the learning process.

In addition, learners set individual goals, monitor their learning, and have greater control over the ways that they demonstrate proficiency and mastery. In each learning experience, learning facilitators and learners co-construct goals that are specific and geared toward mastery of a learning outcome. In Lindsay's Performance Based System, learners have opportunities to personalize or customize their learning plans to meet their academic needs and address their goals and interests.

All learners are expected to engage with advanced learning opportunities that challenge them to strive for level 4 on the four-point scoring scale. Learners may receive these extended or enriched learning opportunities in the regular learning environment (for example, small-group or individualized instruction) or outside it (for example, through community-based learning, internships, or technology). Level 4 learning often involves the application of knowledge and can take place anywhere, anytime, for any learner. Because Lindsay's Performance Based System is not bound by time, age, or grade level, learners can accelerate through the required learning and have opportunities for more rigorous and challenging learning opportunities. Learning facilitators can tailor learning plans for accelerated learning, including faster-paced instruction.

A culture that values the learner's voice is a critical piece of a system that empowers and values learners. Personalized learning plans can address academic, socioemotional, and personal goals and provide an entry point for learners to become invested in the process of their own learning. Lindsay Unified is producing learners who have a more central role in their learning. Learners who, in a more traditional time-based system, might have not been motivated to succeed have been re-engaged.

Differentiation

The district's Performance Based System is grounded in the foundational principle that each learner is unique, with individual needs, interests, learning preferences, and learning styles. Building from assessment data, Lindsay Unified's learning facilitators are able to customize instruction to meet learners at their current levels of proficiency and to offer multiple avenues for learning. This built-in personalization facilitates further differentiation for learners who have more significant needs. Thus, the system is designed to address the diversity that exists among learners, including those with disabilities, English learners, struggling learners, and gifted and talented learners.

For learners who have gaps in their learning or who require additional focused instruction or varied structures, an individual learning plan (ILP) is created—much like an individual education plan (IEP) in special education. An ILP provides an entry point for tailoring learning opportunities and creating differentiation to address learner needs. When working with learners for whom gaps in essential skills and knowledge have been identified, or who need assistance in meeting learning targets in a timely manner, learning facilitators help them construct an ILP. These learners receive various forms of additional instruction to supplement the instructional cycle that all learners participate in. Learning facilitators, specialists, or other learners provide additional support both in and out of class and, in some instances, via technology. In-class supports might include grouping learners who have similar needs, providing explicit direct instruction, focusing on skill-based instruction, or modifying curricula. More intensive structures include increasing instructional time in English language arts and mathematics. Learners may also receive special education services if they are identified as needing specialized services beyond the additional instruction and modified structures.

While developing English language proficiency may be a cause for differentiation, English learners make up a large percentage of Lindsay Unified's learner population; therefore, the district provides linguistic support for all learners. Language support is not simply an add-on to instruction; it is an essential part of all teaching. For example, all measurement topics feature the academic vocabulary required to address the learning targets. In addition, learning facilitators ensure that instruction provides ample opportunities for learners to have content-focused, supported discussions to practice academic language.

The Role of Technology

Lindsay Unified's Technology Vision

- Every learner has access to technology and the Internet at school and at home.

- All Lindsay Unified curricula can be accessed online 24/7, and learners have two or three learning style choices and two or three learning interest choices for most online instruction.

- Lindsay Unified's informational technology systems allow for easy and effective communication between learning facilitators and parents. Parents, at any time, can access their child's learning records, can get tips on how to help their child, and can view the entire Lindsay Unified curriculum.

- Learning facilitators use technology as one effective accelerator of learning to inspire and challenge their learners.

- All technology purchases—hardware, software, and infrastructure—are made based upon the positive impact that the technology will have on learners.

Source: Lindsay Unified School District, 2007.

Moving to the Performance Based System required Lindsay Unified to rethink the structures and tools that support and enable the daily activities of teaching and learning. Technology has been key to the district's ability to personalize instruction. An essential component of personalized learning in Lindsay Unified is the district's learning management system. Originally, the learning management system was a program called Educate, which was used to communicate measurement topics and learning progressions, score learner performance, and provide learners and their families access to the guaranteed and viable curriculum. Educate served the district's initial needs, but as the Performance Based System developed, district leaders, learning facilitators, and learners identified further opportunities for improvement. As the district recognized the importance of a fully integrated and robust learning management system, it used its experience to develop the current learning management system, Empower. Empower is a digital platform used to store and deliver the curriculum, instruction, and assessments, and to document, track, report, and monitor progress for learners. Through Empower, which is accessible at all times, learners can view personal progress on current learning targets, load evidence, and complete various assessment tasks.

Another feature of Empower is the Learner GPS, a tool with which learners can set goals and track their progress. Like a global positioning system (GPS) that helps travelers navigate, the Learner GPS provides a learning road map so learners know where they are in their learning and can chart next steps. The map establishes a clear plan and helps chart future learning in terms of learning target completion and content level advancement. Once a plan is established, the LMS provides a timeline for learning, and a visual gauge displays the learner's progress and pacing.

For example, a learner who is working on language arts content may log into Empower and access her personal database. Viewing her current content level for language arts, she identifies fourteen different learning targets to master the content. Six of these fourteen targets are accompanied by online learning opportunities. For every one of the six standards with an online learning option, links are provided to resources, such as websites, videos, podcasts, or discussion boards. Her learning facilitator will monitor her learning through the learning management system and will also use face-to-face learning experiences to ensure she meets the other targets. Whether at the elementary or high school level, learners have access to the full range of blended learning through the learning management system and the learning environment.

From a learning facilitator's perspective, Empower enables learners to take ownership of their learning. It supports blended learning by offering opportunities for learners to independently master the less complex learning targets and spend quality time with the learning facilitator on more complex, rigorous content. With the use of Empower, more time is available for teachers to engage in small-group instruction, offer in-class coaching, and provide feedback. In addition, many learning facilitators use technology tools, including the Google Suite, for communication, collaboration, project-based learning, research, development of presentations, and progress monitoring.

With a system that utilizes technology in such crucial ways, access to the system is critical. Although Lindsay Unified began with only four computers available in each classroom, the district now provides every learner with one-to-one technology that is appropriate for the learner's age and developmental learning level. This supports the vision of constant and personalized learning. Learning facilitators use flexible classroom structures and furnishings to support digital learning. Lindsay Unified has also begun introducing learning labs replete with technology, which have sliding walls that learning facilitators can reconfigure to accommodate small- or whole-group instruction, labs, or independent study. In these 21st century learning labs, learning facilitators can team-teach and use technology in a variety of ways.

Harnessing the Power of the Internet

The Internet is an important technology tool for the Performance Based System. With appropriate access, the Internet offers nearly unlimited possibilities for ensuring a customized learning experience. Videos, podcasts, tutorials, college classes, and social media are easily available. Well-established programs available through the Internet offer high-quality content for learners and opportunities to self-assess and receive feedback through short quizzes and other automated assignments. The Internet also offers opportunities to differentiate instruction for advanced learners through online advanced placement (AP) courses.

The district offers Internet hotspots that are open to all parents and learners. In addition, Lindsay Unified provides communitywide Wi-Fi by establishing a network of hotspots throughout the community so learners and families can access education programs anytime, anywhere. Without this Internet access provided by the district, many families would not have access outside of school. Learners now commonly use technology throughout the learning community, and adults use devices to build shared curricula, analyze data, and manage all communications and initiatives.

Learning to Use Technology

A substantial challenge to implementing Lindsay Unified's Performance Based System was ensuring that both learners and adults were able to effectively use the district's technology tools. As time goes on, more and more students arrive in the classroom as digital natives, having grown up using computers, smartphones, and the Internet. It is the responsibility of learning facilitators and other staff, however, to ensure that all learners and adults are proficient with technology and are using it in ways that best serve the learning. All teaching staff participate in professional development on using the technology tools that are now essential to the system. Regular community-based workshops are conducted to train parents on how to access learner records, monitor progress, and support learning.

Lindsay Unified also provides hands-on workshops for learners to develop the technology skills to access learning targets, engage with online curricula, take assessments, and monitor progress. Once learners have demonstrated proficiency in digital citizenship and the norms of utilizing technology appropriately, ethically, and productively, mobile devices are distributed for use both at school and at home.

Summary

In the scope of the transformation in Lindsay Unified, it was imperative to renovate and re-envision teaching and learning at all levels. Based on the most pertinent research and theory, district and site leadership, alongside learning facilitators, crafted a system of teaching and learning that changed the outcomes in the classroom and the expectations of learners. This system, derived from the philosophy of the strategic design, harnessed the power of personalization to inspire learner empowerment and accountability and develop critical integrations of technology. Learners, once uninspired by the act of daily learning, became active partners in their learning and recipients of a 21st century education.

Instructional transformations in Lindsay Unified involved the following aspects.

- Embracing the systems of learning
- Implementing a cycle of instruction
- Adopting and utilizing research-based practices

To better engage students in the learning process, the district implemented the following strategies.

- Involving learners in the creation of norms and protocols
- Developing a growth mindset in learners
- Empowering learners to set and achieve goals

Technology, a crucial tool for the Performance Based System, was incorporated by the district in the following ways.

- Developing a plan for technology integration
- Harnessing the power of the Internet
- Expanding access to technology programs and services
- Training staff and learners in all aspects of technology

Tania

Tania struggled with her acquisition of English. As a young child, before Lindsay's Performance Based System, she struggled through English as a second language classes and felt very little learning had any value. In Lindsay Unified's Performance Based System, Tania was introduced to a new system of learning.

Two of the most immediate changes she noticed were the clear expectations for learning and the new uses of technology. Rather than scheduling her more time in English language development classes, she had a learning facilitator who monitored her development of English in small-group instruction and through web-based programs that Tania could also work on at home. In addition, through multimodal instruction, Tania discovered she could be successful in subjects that had once been hard for her. She thrived in her science and art classes and began to seek more support in her learning goals in English language arts and mathematics.

At home, she shared her successes with her family and began to tutor her younger siblings in their English language development. Tania's acquisition of English grew rapidly, and after three years of the new system of learning, she was reclassified from her status as an English learner.

CHAPTER 7

Introducing the Lindsay Community Today

Lindsay Unified's Stakeholder Vision

- The goals, vision, and values of the district are a direct reflection of the broader Lindsay community. The Lindsay community helped to set the Strategic Plan for their schools, so there is natural community support for the district's vision and values.

- Lindsay Unified values and encourages parent participation that reflects the cultural diversity of the community.

- Members of the broader Lindsay community are very familiar with and supportive of the district's vision. . . . Education is a top priority for everyone. It is common to see parents in Lindsay learning communities providing additional learning opportunities to children and youth.

- Lindsay parents are supportive of learning facilitators and of their children's learning communities, and they team with schools to ensure that their children receive the best education possible.

continued ➜

- Lindsay Unified facilities are first rate. All learning environments are clean, inviting, and suited for learning.

- Because the learning outcomes for Lindsay Unified schools are "life-based," it is natural that the community serves as a learning laboratory for the school. Adults mentor children, businesses open their facilities for learning, and business/school partnerships allow learners to experience the real world. Parent involvement is integral to learner achievement in the system developed by Lindsay Unified. Parents and guardians are a child's first and most influential learning facilitators.

Source: Lindsay Unified School District, 2007.

Throughout the transformation to the Performance Based System, Lindsay Unified has prioritized the inclusion of a wide range of stakeholders. Learners' lives and educational needs are impacted by the community in which they live, while the school system and the graduates it produces have an equally strong impact on the community. These facts are the driving force behind Lindsay's efforts to integrate the educational system with the community as much as possible. One aspect of this aim is proactively including learners' parents and guardians.

Parents reinforce the value of learning and serve as key motivators in their children's lives. At home, parents foster growth in literacy, accountability, and lifelong learning. Most important, children look to their parents for support in learning experiences that are new and challenging, and as such, Lindsay Unified works actively to ensure parents are key stakeholders in decisions and opportunities regarding their children's learning. Sustained parental involvement contributes greatly to learner achievement and fosters a positive school environment. The district works closely with each site administrator and various program directors (migrant services, after school programs, student services, and so on) to coordinate all parent involvement and training efforts so that parents are prepared to be involved in the learning community and in their children's education. When parents invest in and support the activities of the learning community, the trust and continuity established lead to better learning opportunities and outcomes.

Lindsay Unified provides a variety of workshops to empower parents to provide their children with academic support in the home. These workshops include Parent University, Digital Citizenship, All About the Performance Based System, Supporting Learning at Home, Family Digital Literacy, LUSD 1-to-One World Initiative, and Math and Literacy Family Fun Night. In addition, parents receive training on how to access and use the LMS to monitor their children's progress. The district also offers English as a second language classes for adults, targeting families of English learners and families of immigrant learners. The program provides three hours of classroom instruction twice a week to as many as twenty-five adults. The main focus is to develop parents' English proficiency so they can assist in their children's overall academic achievement, but the program also gives parents specific strategies for becoming more involved in their children's education.

Learner and parent empowerment are an indispensable part of ensuring transformation and the success of Lindsay's Performance Based System. Built as a network of supports and opportunities, the community's diversity, socioeconomic needs, and cultural values are at the forefront of supporting learners and their families.

Next, we will discuss Lindsay's Healthy Start Family Resource Center, the significance of a Migrant Education Program (specifically Lindsay's designation as Migrant Education Region 24), and the way the larger Lindsay community serves as a learning laboratory itself.

Healthy Start Family Resource Center

With a clear awareness that learners can only learn when they are healthy, feel safe, and have their other basic needs met, Lindsay Unified sought opportunities to provide integrated, comprehensive support services. With poor access to health and related services, the community needed trusted resources to connect families to mental health, dental, and medical care.

In 1994, Lindsay Unified School District opened its Healthy Start Family Resource Center (HSFRC), collaborating closely with school staff to ensure that learners and families have access to necessary mental and physical health services. In a poverty-stricken community like

Lindsay, access to health and related services is limited by geographical, linguistic, and cultural barriers. Providing comprehensive services to learners and their families meets a critical need in supporting their school attendance, productivity, stability, and achievement.

Comprehensive case-managed services ensure connectivity with the best resources as well as a reduction in the duplication of services. As appropriate, families are referred to agencies for specialized assistance with basic needs, such as utility credits, bus tokens, temporary housing, food vouchers, clothing, and baby supplies. In addition, a variety of evidence-based parenting curricula is offered, including Parenting Wisely, Safe Care, Fresh Start, Eating Well/Living Well, Nurturing Parent, and Opening Doors, all of which are geared toward enhancing parents' participation in their children's education. The HSFRC also coordinates efforts among several public agencies to provide therapeutic services to Lindsay learners and families needing such care. These services include infant care, domestic violence counseling, parent and child interactive therapy, and substance-abuse counseling. In sum, HSFRC prepares and supports Lindsay learners before they walk in the door of the learning community, takes care of Lindsay learners when they leave the learning community each day, and supports Lindsay learners throughout the community. Parents help shape the program by providing valuable feedback about what is lacking in the Lindsay community. The feedback is used to seek additional funding opportunities that will support Lindsay families and children.

The Lindsay Diabetes Project is an example of strong commitment to Lindsay learners by the broader community. Supported by the Lindsay District Hospital Board, but integrated as an initiative of HSFRC, the project is focused on assisting with the prevention and management of diabetes, a growing health concern in the Lindsay community, where the diabetes rate is nearly double the regional, state, and national averages. The Lindsay Diabetes Project involves dozens of people from local and regional hospitals and multiple health care agencies.

Lindsay families have come to trust and rely on the HSFRC. The broad range of resources it encompasses provides essential support for the health of children and their families in the community.

Migrant Education Region 24

The community of Lindsay is designated as Migrant Education Region 24, and more than 1,200 migrant families in the community receive services through the California Department of Education's Migrant Education Program. The following supplemental services, offered to migrant families, are designed to level the playing field and ensure migrant learners have the opportunity to excel in school.

- **Preschool:** Provides opportunities for language development, socioemotional learning, early literacy, and school adjustment for three- and four-year-olds

- **In-home parenting courses:** Provides learning opportunities for parents to improve their understanding of child development, health, nutrition, play, safety, and healthy discipline

- **Family literacy:** Provides materials and training that support parents working with their children to develop literacy skills

- **Representation at the State Migrant Parent Conference:** Provides training and development for migrant parent leaders

- **University of Southern California Mobile Dental Clinic:** Provides free dental services, including prevention and treatment for all dental needs

- **Supplemental academic programs and services:** Provides tutoring and interventions to supplement regular learning opportunities

- **Specialized extracurricular activities:** Provides leadership opportunities and conferences for learners, exploratory learning, migrant learner debates, and family activities

- **Support from the Mexican consulate:** Provides links to medical services, citizenship classes, documentation, and legal representation

The Migrant Education Program is instrumental in helping all Lindsay learners succeed.

The Community as Curriculum

Part of Lindsay Unified's vision for its stakeholders is that the larger Lindsay community serves as a learning laboratory. Because of its belief that learning should happen both within and outside the classroom, the district has worked to establish a myriad of community-based learning opportunities. Industry and business partnerships play an important role in these efforts through advisory committees, curriculum development, and the provision of learning opportunities. Learners can obtain work experience, hands-on training in various industries, and opportunities to test out fields of interest before committing to college or a career. Community partnerships also provide resources for college-to-career sustainability. Additionally, Lindsay learners have access to real-life, outside-the-classroom learning opportunities through such projects as Partnerships With Proteus, the Workforce Investment Board, Jobs for the Future, Tulare-Kings Linked Learning Consortium, and a variety of other businesses in the community that partner with the district. These community-based learning experiences include both paid and unpaid short-term opportunities for Lindsay learners to work with industry professionals. For example, high school learners in Lindsay have opportunities to complete internships related to their college- or career-focused coursework. The community members who open their businesses to learners serve as mentors and communicate with learning facilitators and site personnel to ensure continuous growth.

The community is also an integral part of the annual senior project for graduating high school learners. All seniors engage with the community as part of their required curriculum. They organize and participate in a job shadow in a local business and complete a project to reflect on the experience. As part of their culminating presentations, seniors are prompted to consider if, based on those work experiences, the fields they plan to enter are a good fit. For example, seniors who envision themselves as nurses must learn, on the job, if they are prepared to complete the daily work of a nurse. These presentations—evaluated by a panel of business owners, educators, and city personnel—require graduating seniors to present the results of their job shadow, their successes and challenges in the Performance Based System, and future plans with detail and forethought. The community panelists consider how well the Performance Based System served seniors and whether they are prepared for the plans they have outlined.

Further evidence of the broader community's commitment to Lindsay learners is the close partnership between the district and the city of Lindsay. As part of Lindsay Unified's after-school program, learners go to the McDermont Field House, a city-operated recreation facility that has indoor fields and courts, a fitness center, and other activities. The partnership allows for implementation of various recreation, nutrition, and academic programs for Lindsay learners, in alignment with the district's vision and supported by contracts between the city and the district.

In addition, Lindsay Unified partners with the city to share the funding for a school resource officer (SRO) who is dedicated to Lindsay learners and families during the school year. The SRO helps build and reinforce the concept that law enforcement officials are partners with the district in serving and protecting individuals and the community. The SRO spends a significant amount of time building positive relationships with Lindsay learners and families and has become a source of strong support for many of them.

Summary

The Lindsay community continues to evolve with the transformation of the district and the implementation of the Performance Based System. Rather than operating as a separate entity, the community actively supports learners and their families in a myriad of ways. Families are provided with a wide range of services including those that serve their basic needs, cultural and linguistic support, and continued academic and literacy experiences. Learners benefit from the community as a curricular platform that brings college and career experiences into their daily learning cycles. Rather than only providing what is requisite, the Lindsay community works in tandem with the district to enrich and fulfill the lives of learners and their families.

The entire Lindsay community strengthens the Performance Based System; the district fostered this relationship through the following methods.

- Creating venues of inclusion for all stakeholders, especially parents
- Planning and delivering parent empowerment sessions
- Harnessing the resources of local programs
- Creating community-based learning opportunities

Brian

Brian works hard in his learning to be the first in his family to graduate from high school. His parents, who emigrated from Mexico to Lindsay just after Brian was born, do their best to provide for Brian and his siblings, but their agricultural work often requires that they move frequently and leaves little money for anything beyond necessities.

Because Brian was identified upon his enrollment in Lindsay Unified as a migrant learner with young siblings at home, his family receives services from both the Healthy Start Family Resource Center and the Migrant Education Program. During the course of the year, his mother is able to receive financial support for groceries, warm clothes for the children in winter, classes in parenting, and materials for Brian and his siblings to be successful at school, such as backpacks and notebooks. They also benefit from regular medical and dental appointments and any follow-up care necessary. Without such assistance, Brian's family would struggle to provide the care and support that ensure that Brian and his siblings can learn and achieve their goals.

Epilogue

As would likely be true for any district, the transformation of Lindsay Unified from a traditional time-based education system to the learner-centered Performance Based System was a difficult journey, yielding many lessons learned along the way. While such transformation requires a certain level of courageous leadership and risk taking, it also requires very intentional and calculated strategic action to dismantle traditional systems and structures and replace them with learner-centered systems and structures. This work can be most effectively carried out through a process similar to the instructional cycle—by setting goals, carefully analyzing results, gathering feedback from stakeholders, responding to feedback with necessary changes, and repeating the cycle.

Following are five key considerations for any school or district beginning the transformation to performance-based learning. These considerations, based on lessons learned, should be given significant attention by everyone involved in any planning process, as they are critical to advancing efforts to transform education by personalizing learning.

1. **Involve learners from the very beginning:** Valuing the voice of the learner up front leads to greater levels of learner empowerment and more effective problem solving. Many learners know better than adults how to fix the system. Involve them in the development of the strategic design. When making decisions, bring learner leadership teams into the process whenever possible.

When faced with problems in the transformation, ask the learners, "How should we get there?" or "What would you recommend?" Learners often recognize problems with the traditional system better than anyone because they have been living those problems every day during their schooling. Honor and utilize the voices of learners to build the case for change and to lead the transformation.

2. **Clearly establish the expectation that all members of the leadership team will use the strategic design as the guiding document for the transformation:** The strategic design is the collective voice of the community that the leaders serve. If all leaders do not understand and use the strategic design in their daily work, the entire vision will be placed to the side and forgotten. The strategic design needs to be a document that all leaders embrace and live by if they are to lead in the organization. Such commitment by leaders causes a significant acceleration toward realization of the vision. Transformation becomes possible when leaders at all levels—from the school board to the superintendent to the principals, directors, and coordinators—teach the strategic design components to their staff, infuse the strategic design into all professional development, include it in all of their communications, personally live the core values, and hold others accountable for doing the same. Leaders who are not committed to the mission and vision of the organization need to move out of the way and let others lead, so that learners can really learn.

3. **Make the strategic design the centerpiece for the entire community early on:** The strategic design document should not become an internal document used only by administrators or those in leadership positions; it must be integrated into the work of all staff from the very beginning. Such focus will lead to greater alignment of all efforts across the learning community. What people do, what decisions are made, how funds are spent, and many other foundational aspects of the organization come into closer alignment when the strategic design is fully embraced by all. Taking intentional action to educate all stakeholders on the

key components of the strategic design has been critical to ensuring that staff, parents, and the community more clearly understand and embrace the transformation. The strategic design should become a valued guiding document to all staff and to many learners and parents. When embraced and lived out by all stakeholders, the vision gives people a higher level of purpose in their roles and becomes an intrinsic motivator. Uniting around a common mission and vision (as outlined in the strategic design) creates clarity in the daily work and keeps priorities in focus.

4. **Make lifelong learning standards part of the core curriculum from the very beginning of curriculum development work:** To ensure that learners become highly motivated, self-directed, and fully empowered to take ownership of their learning, standards for lifelong learning should be valued to the same degree as reading, writing, and math. Lifelong learning standards, which define what a community wants its graduates to be like, should be the backbone of all learning in a personalized, learner-centered system. When Lindsay Unified started its transformation to the Performance Based System, the power and importance of its lifelong learning standards were not fully understood or appreciated. As the district evolved in its transformation, it was apparent that these critical socioemotional competencies were integrally tied to how learners engaged in learning and progressed academically.

5. **Remain focused on the intended outcome of a performance-based system (all learners reaching their full academic and personal potential):** In the transformation process, it is easy to get overwhelmed with completing discrete tasks and implementing pieces of the system and lose track of the main goal, which is to produce high levels of learner achievement. Therefore, being relentless in the drive to produce academic achievement and personal success for learners—a results-driven culture of accountability—is essential. When engaging in transformational work, it is critical not to lose sight of the obligation to produce learning results.

The journey does not end when the transition to a performance-based model of education is complete, however. Sustaining the system requires constant work, continuous adaptation, and a future-focused mindset. Lindsay Unified's plans for the future include the following three.

1. **Completing the adult curriculum:** The district will complete the final build-out of the adult curriculum, which is the curriculum that describes the knowledge, skills, and dispositions that learning facilitators, principals, superintendents, and school board members need in order to lead a results-driven, performance-based learning community. The adult curriculum will provide clarity about the knowledge and skills required, and will also provide the resources that will enable all adults in the system to drive their own learning.

2. **Creating a stronger, results-driven culture:** Lindsay Unified will support implementation of additional engagement strategies that keep all learners invested in their learning and wanting to learn more. Site-based teams will plan, monitor, and adjust instruction to ensure achievement of learning goals.

3. **Creating opportunities to embrace learning:** Lindsay Unified's future-focused drive will ensure that all Lindsay learners have opportunities to embrace rigorous, relevant learning through a variety of venues, especially through technology, as the district nears the completion of the communitywide Wi-Fi project. Opportunities for learners to reach level 4 mastery, including community-based projects, college- and career-level learning, and internships will continue to create open-walled learning experiences. In addition, continuous access to the Internet will make learning possible anywhere and anytime for Lindsay learners.

From day one of its transformation effort, Lindsay Unified has focused on its mission, and as it continues to strengthen and sustain its learner-centered Performance Based System, the district's work will continue to be guided by that same mission: Empowering and Motivating for Today and Tomorrow.

Appendix

Visit **marzanoresearch.com/reproducibles** to download these resources.

The following strategies and checklists will be helpful as you make your own systemic changes.

Recommended Strategies for Ensuring a Successful Transformation

- Collaborate with all stakeholders to develop a future-focused strategic design.

- Invest the time and energy to create a unified mission and vision.

- Develop collective ownership of the mission and vision.

- Use consistent messaging to sustain focus on the mission and vision.

- Identify the systems and components required for the new model.

- Focus on developing the leadership skills needed for transformational change.

- Learn and engage in effective teamwork practices.

- Make lifelong learning outcomes part of the core curriculum.

- Maintain a relentless focus on results, especially improved learner achievement.

- Center communication and goal setting around learner achievement.

Checklist for Shifting to a Performance-Based System

Following is a checklist to aid your own shift from a traditional system to Lindsay's Performance Based System.

Creating Preliminary Change

- [ ] Address immediate business and organizational issues.
- [ ] Build leadership capacity.
- [ ] Build harmonious relationships with staff.
- [ ] Ensure that the board of trustees understands and supports the reform efforts.
- [ ] Improve instructional practices.
- [ ] Seek out research-based practices and outside perspectives.
- [ ] Engage key stakeholders in jointly developing a strategic design.

Creating a New Culture

- [ ] Develop a set of core values.
- [ ] Establish guiding principles and beliefs.
- [ ] Enact a visionary vocabulary.
- [ ] Adopt a mastery mindset.
- [ ] Define the ideal graduate.
- [ ] Identify socioemotional competencies for graduates.

Transforming Leadership

- [ ] Develop strategic direction and alignment.
- [ ] Develop and empower leadership.
- [ ] Focus on professional outcomes and organizational health.
- [ ] Develop core value rubrics for leadership.

Transforming Personnel

☐ Develop core values for all personnel.

☐ Align all personnel to core values.

☐ Develop a new mindset for all staff.

☐ Provide support and training.

Transforming Curricula

☐ Define essential learning.

☐ Develop measurement topics.

☐ Develop rubrics and progressions.

☐ Activate learners at appropriate content levels.

☐ Develop socioemotional learning outcomes.

Transforming Assessment

☐ Integrate assessments with the instructional model.

☐ Determine assessment types.

☐ Determine instructional uses for assessments.

☐ Correlate assessments to scoring scales.

Transforming Teaching

☐ Embrace the systems of learning.

☐ Implement a cycle of instruction.

☐ Adopt and utilize research-based practices.

Transforming Learning

☐ Involve learners in the creation of norms and protocols.

☐ Develop a growth mindset in learners.

☐ Empower learners to set and achieve goals.

Transforming Technology

- ☐ Develop a plan for technology integration.
- ☐ Harness the power of the Internet.
- ☐ Expand access to technology programs and services.
- ☐ Train staff and learners in all aspects of technology.

Connecting With the Community

- ☐ Create venues of inclusion for all stakeholders, especially parents.
- ☐ Plan and deliver parent empowerment sessions.
- ☐ Harness the resources of local programs.
- ☐ Create community-based learning opportunities.

References

Bellanca, J., & Brandt, R. (Eds.). (2010). *21st century skills: Rethinking how students learn*. Bloomington, IN: Solution Tree Press.

California Department of Education. (2001, September 28). *1999 Base API - Data File*. Accessed at www3.cde.ca.gov/researchfiles/api /api99btx.zip on June 30, 2016.

California Department of Education. (2006, December 21). *2004-05 Growth API - Data File (TXT)*. Accessed at www3.cde.ca.gov /researchfiles/api/api05gtx.zip on June 28, 2016.

California Department of Education. (2016, May 17). *Unduplicated student poverty—Free or reduced price meals data 2015–16*. Accessed at www .cde.ca.gov/ds/sd/sd/filessp.asp on June 28, 2016.

California Department of Education Data Reporting Office. (n.d.). *English learner students by language by grade, 5471993 Lindsay Unified 2015–16*. Accessed at http://data1.cde.ca.gov/dataquest/SpringData /StudentsByLanguage.aspx?Level=District&TheYear=2015-16& SubGroup=All&ShortYear=1516&GenderGroup=B&CDSCode= 54719930000000&RecordType=EL on June 28, 2016.

Dweck, C. S. (2006). *Mindset: The new psychology of success*. New York: Random House.

Fadel, C., Bialik, M., & Trilling, B. (2015). *Four-dimensional education: The competencies learners need to succeed*. Boston: Center for Curriculum Redesign.

Hattie, J. (2012). *Visible learning for teachers: Maximizing impact on learning*. New York: Routledge.

Lencioni, P. (2002). *The five dysfunctions of a team: A leadership fable*. San Francisco: Jossey-Bass.

Lencioni, P. (2012). *The advantage: Why organizational health trumps everything else in business*. San Francisco: Jossey-Bass.

Lindsay Unified School District. (2007). *LUSD strategic design*. Accessed at www.lindsay.k12.ca.us/filelibrary/LUSD%20Strategic%20Design%201.pdf on October 6, 2016.

Marzano, R. J. (1992). *A different kind of classroom: Teaching with dimensions of learning*. Alexandria, VA: Association for Supervision and Curriculum Development.

Marzano, R. J. (2003). *What works in schools: Translating research into action*. Alexandria, VA: Association for Supervision and Curriculum Development.

Marzano, R. J. (2007). *The art and science of teaching: A comprehensive framework for effective instruction*. Alexandria, VA: Association for Supervision and Curriculum Development.

Marzano, R. J. (2009). *Designing & teaching learning goals & objectives*. Bloomington, IN: Marzano Research.

Marzano, R. J. (with Boogren, T. H., Heflebower, T., Kanold-McIntyre, J., & Pickering, D. J.) (2012). *Becoming a reflective teacher*. Bloomington, IN: Marzano Research.

Marzano, R. J., & Kendall, J. S. (2007). *The new taxonomy of educational objectives* (2nd ed.). Thousand Oaks, CA: Corwin Press.

Marzano, R. J., Norford, J. S., Paynter, D. E., Pickering, D. J., & Gaddy, B. B. (2001). *A handbook for classroom instruction that works*. Alexandria, VA: Association for Supervision and Curriculum Development.

Marzano, R. J., & Pickering, D. J. (1997). *Dimensions of learning: Teacher's manual* (2nd ed.). Alexandria, VA: Association for Supervision and Curriculum Development.

Marzano, R. J., Pickering, D. J., & Pollock, J. E. (2001). *Classroom instruction that works: Research-based strategies for increasing student achievement*. Alexandria, VA: Association for Supervision and Curriculum Development.

Pancoast, M. (2011). *The breakthrough coach management development for instructional leaders Malachi Pancoast*. Accessed at www.the-breakthrough-coach.com/ on June 28, 2016.

Schwahn, C., & McGarvey, B. (2011). *Inevitable: Mass customized learning—Learning in the age of empowerment*. (n.p.): Authors.

Schwahn, C., & McGarvey, B. (with Crawford, P., Rearick, D., & Scott, J.). (2014). *Inevitable too!: The total leader embraces mass customized learning.* (n.p.): Authors.

Schwahn, C. J., & Spady, W. G. (2010). *Total leaders 2.0: Leading in the age of empowerment.* Lanham, MD: Rowman & Littlefield Education.

Index